Reviews for Kevin Norley's books

'*Making Britain Literate* and *Making Britain Numerate* cover key requirements for teaching basic literacy and numeracy. Suitable for professional teachers and homeschoolers, both books include helpful examples and exercises.'

Newsletter No 70, Spring 2010, Campaign for Real Education

'I recently passed both my L2 literacy and numeracy at Bedford College. I found the ideas contained in both Mr Norley's books really useful. I developed a better understanding of English (which is my second language), particularly with the grammar, which even helped me with my maths.'

Marilyn L (Bedford College, June 2010)

'(Making Britain Numerate) is a superb book which can be used as a study guide for anyone wishing to improve their own numeracy skills, or help someone else with theirs. I have used it with many of my staff and all have commented at how easy it is to grasp the concepts within it. All have shown improvements in their numeracy skills.'

S.W., Area Manager, East of England, March 2009, Amazon.co.uk

'I have recently finished a maths course at the Luton Learning Centre. There were 15 of us on the course, from all different parts of the world. Kevin showed us very clearly how to work with fractions and percentages, how to convert from one to the other, and how those conversions can be used to both better understand and solve problems including those involving scale and volume. His explanations were detailed, and he had high expectations of all of us. Needless to say, I achieved my L2 numeracy qualification.'

Caroline O (Luton Learning Centre, July '10)

'I needed a level 2 numeracy qualification in order to be accepted onto a BSc Social Work and Mental Health Nursing degree course, so I attended a numeracy workshop at the Skillsbank. The resources used and methods taught from 'Making Britain Numerate' were very straightforward and ideal for ensuring that I obtained my qualification quickly!'

Charity M (Bedford College, June '10)

Making Britain Literate

Kevin Norley

Imprimata

Published by **Imprimata**

A CIP Catalogue record for this book is available from the British Library

ISBN 978-1-906192-38-9

Printed in Great Britain

Imprimata Publishers Limited
www.imprimata.co.uk

I would like to dedicate this book
to my mother and to my wife.

How is English used today?

"I done it before. I rit it there!" exclaimed Sarah, her softly spoken voice raising a pitch and taking me back slightly, but not enough to stall my retort, as I had anticipated it.

"Uh I think you mean 'I did it before. I wrote it there'" I said calmly, smiling. Sensing no adverse reaction, I continued.

"Just tell me something, Sarah. You recently spent 11 years in state schools from 5 – 16, right."

"uh huh"

"During that time, did anyone at your school or in your home environment, or anyone for that matter, correct your English?"

"Maybe… I don't know… I guess not." she replied with a nervous smile.

"That's o.k." I said. "Don't worry about it. I mean many people in our society speak the same way" I continued, in a rather apologetic tone. "It's not a big deal". I wanted to be quick to play it down, not to make her feel bad in any way.

Sarah was in a way the ideal person to 'experiment' on, to prove to myself what I already knew. She was one of the brighter learners in the class, quiet and good natured. She was coming to the end of her 8 week short intensive basic skills programme, one of the programmes designed for unemployed people sent to the training organisation I worked for by the job centre to improve her literacy and numeracy skills. She'd progressed well with her level 1 adult literacy and numeracy, and would take her L1 tests soon and move on. The environment was ideal too. A small class of unemployed adults, individuals, each with their own difficulties in life, their own issues, but no group mentality, generally passive and subdued. What's more, they were used to my social class foibles, reminding them to pronounce their 't's, 'th's and 'h's, to say you 'were' not you 'was', not to use double negatives etc. They were also used to me nagging them about the importance of reading as much as possible in order to improve their literacy and increase their everyday vocabulary.

How was I able to get away with this? Well, for a while I was their teacher, and having built up a good relationship with the students, I could get away with trying. It wasn't easy though, nor was I successful 'Why does it matter how I speak?' 'That's how my mum speaks', 'Everyone else speaks like this', 'I don't want to talk posh'. I was familiar with that one, and would often counter that there weren't just two ways of speaking i.e. 'street language' and 'posh', that there was plain 'ole standard English too, although not to much avail, as I was aware that this was often perceived as 'posh' too. It was difficult to win an argument or convince anyone of the need to speak standard English, or what I was trying to portray as 'correct' grammar and pronunciation, and they must have wondered why I bothered. I would emphasise however that I believed that people should feel free to express themselves the way they want to, but that at the same time they needed to know how and when to use standard English. I didn't expect them to 'talk posh' when they were having a drink with their friends, but I expected them to know, in an educational or professional environment, how to utilise standard English for their own advantage.

I would also emphasise that the way in which any member of a social group converses, and the pronunciation they use, will depend upon the situation they're in. The variety of language then that any member uses that is appropriate for that particular situation is known as a *register*. For example, when doctors explain problems to patients, they try to avoid the medical, specialised terms, so that they can make themselves understood. However, the same ideas will be conveyed in a different, more technical language when those doctors are discussing the cases with their colleagues. Another example could be the language used by TV presenters. During broadcasting they are likely to use standard English and received pronunciation (RP). However, the same people will speak in a different way while having a drink with their friends, or while playing with their children. These examples then serve to illustrate the relationship between contextual language and social group.

The English language has been subject to a multitude of influences over the years, and has inevitably changed with time. There has been much written about how, and the extent to which language has evolved over time, and the main influences on the language (e.g. Knowles 1997, Hughes and Trudgill 1979). It would be fair then to say that language use within any of the social groups that make up the English speaking population has changed over the years, and is therefore not fixed. However, I would argue that language use itself is determined by the social groups in which we live, and that although it changes, differences remain between the language use of those social groups, and that those differences in language use in turn, determine the the social group we belong to. This fact is highlighted by Kramsch (1998: 3) for example, who explains that 'members of a… social group do not only express experience; they also create experience through language', and goes on to argue that:

> The way in which people use the spoken, written, or visual medium itself creates meanings that are understandable to the group they belong to …
>
> **(Kramsch 1998: 3)**

In terms of the social groups themselves, Gardiner (2003) states that:

> Examples of social groups that might be said to have their own distinctive styles of language use include those based on socio-economic status, age, occupation and gender.'
>
> **(Gardiner 2003:32)**

There has been a lot of research into the extent to which language use is affected by which social group one belongs to. Gardiner (2003: 33) outlines briefly the effects of the above-mentioned social groups on language use when, for example, he writes about how some occupations have their ''own specialist vocabulary' or 'jargon', how women and men 'use language in different ways' and how speech differs between 'teenagers' and 'older members of the same community.'

This specialist vocabulary can be said to reinforce a profession or trade's identity and help its members to communicate with greater clarity, economy and precision. The legal, medical, IT and teaching professions are examples of professions that use quite specialist vocabulary. Using specialist vocabulary can however give the users a feeling of self importance and serve to exclude people from outside a particular profession or trade. In terms of gender, it has been found that women's accents are less pronounced and that their language generally tends more towards standard English than men's. Also, research has shown that men are more assertive and less co-operative than women in conversational interaction. This can be demonstrated through observing how men 'butt in' more often during conversations, and swear more often (Eames and Wainwright 1999). In terms of age, teenagers and young people in general have a large and ever changing lexicon of slang words and colloquialisms which strengthen their identity as a social group. Knowles (1997: 5) makes an analogy between young people adopting 'new styles of speech' and 'new styles of dress and other social habits.' Furthermore, people of all generations often stick with the informal lexis of their youth e.g. popular words with young people in the sixties included 'pad', 'chick' and 'pot', whilst in the nineties they included 'eco-warriors', 'surfing the net' and 'spin-doctor.'

Socio-economic status shall be looked at shortly, but going back to my students, I appreciated the fact that if they had left school and were speaking with such grammar, there wasn't a lot that I could do, in effective isolation and in a short period of time. I was also aware that this was just one of many examples of how the argument for the importance and relevance for the use of standard spoken English had been lost. I would show newspaper articles on the importance of the spoken word, how employers decry the slovenly decline of the spoken word amongst the youth, and how it affects their job opportunities etc. I would be careful to portray it as 'just someone else's view and move on quickly. I was aware that the reasons these guys didn't work went well beyond the way they spoke. I was just trying to illustrate it as a factor.

Wind forward a few years. I was attending a 3 day teachers' conference entitled 'Teaching the Teacher Trainer' in which the main focus was the delivery of new teaching qualifications (Preparing to Teach in the Lifelong Learning Sector (PTLLS), Certificate in Teaching in the Lifelong Learning Sector (CTLLS) and the Diploma in Teaching in the Lifelong Learning Sector (DTLLS)) in relation to new standards. The conference included several useful workshops such as, 'The role of the teacher educator', 'Approaches to teaching and learning',

'Reflective practice' and 'Principles of effective feedback'. As part of one the workshops, we were split into groups of 5, and given the task of preparing a short (15 minute) presentation reflecting on how we would deliver an element of the new standards for the literacy and/or ESOL subject specialisms for the DTLLS. My chosen element was an analysis of the personal, social and cultural factors influencing literacy learners' development of spoken and written language. Within this area then, I chose to focus on the teaching and learning of grammar in relation to social class, and in the context of, developing speaking and listening, and writing skills, of adult learners.

So, I began my presentation by outlining my objectives along with some supportive theory upon which I was to base some of my arguments. The plan was then to outline, based on my experience, and with practical examples, why I felt the teaching of Standard English through constant and consistent error correction of grammar and pronunciation was important in improving learners' speaking and listening skills and how doing so would give them a wider base upon which to develop other literacy skills. This was to be done in the context of acknowledging the potential difficulties and awkwardness of correcting adults' speech and subtle ways in which this could be addressed. With this in mind, the argument was to be set against what I believe to be the prevailing orthodoxy in many educational environments relating to spoken grammar and pronunciation i.e. to accept equally all forms of spoken grammatical variations related to socio-economic group and region. Following this, the arguments were to be opened up for discussion.

Leading on from my introduction, I highlighted the afore-mentioned comment, 'I done it before. I rit it there', as an example of the common use of non-standard English which in my opinion should have been anticipated and not allowed to develop within the eleven years of a pupil's educational experience but which should still nevertheless be corrected if used as an adult (or post-16) learner. Within the time limitation that I had, I didn't plan to discuss or even touch upon pronunciation. The general trend was that while someone was presenting, the others would listen, and only interrupt to seek clarification or supplement the presentation with a supporting comment or anecdote. However, maybe due to the nature of my presentation, this was to change. Following on from my analysis, I was interrupted by one of the course's facilitators with a comment of, 'To me that is standard English'. This provoked a response from me seeking clarification on the comment, which in turn led to a range of views from the group which were broadly critical of the stance I had, till then, been taking. The discussion became slightly heated. Off script, I gave examples of how I thought, generally speaking, that in work environments, one could relate the level of a person's occupation to the way they spoke (i.e. their grammar and pronunciation), which led to another critical comment. I managed to get back on to my presentation and hurried through the remainder of it, although indeed an uncomfortable atmosphere had been created.

In terms of socio-economic status, or social class, there has been much written about the correlation between language use and educational attainment and culture, a lot of which has been the subject of some quite contentious debate. Much of the issue has surrounded the use of 'standard English' and 'non-standard English' dialects, and whether or not the former is 'better' or 'superior' to the latter, and accent variations (the use of 'Received Pronunciation' (RP) as compared with regional non-RP accents). The grammatical and lexical (vocabulary) differences between non-standard British dialects and standard English, along with comparisons between RP and regional non-RP accents are outlined in detail by Hughes and Trudgill (1979) in their study of social and regional varieties of British English. In their study, they define the term 'standard English' as 'the dialect of educated people throughout the British Isles' (1979: 8). Trudgill (1994: 6) puts forward a clear argument that the use of non-standard dialects is, '... not 'wrong' in any way... ' and that the use of non-standard forms:

> '... should not be regarded as 'mistakes'. They are used by millions of English speakers around the world and are representative of grammatical systems that are different from Standard English, not linguistically inferior to it.'
>
> **(Trudgill 1994: 6)**

In contrast to this, Honey (1997) in his book 'Language is Power', argues that schools have been failing working-class and ethnic minority children through not insisting on the exclusive use of standard English, and states that:

> '... to give access to standard English to those members of society who have not acquired facility in it through their parents, is an important priority in any society concerned with social justice and the reduction of educational inequalities.'
>
> **(Honey 1997: 5)**

When considered alongside a claim from Clark and Ivanic (1997: 55) that schools' literacy policies exclude 'powerless social groups... from contributing to the collective store of knowledge, cultural and ideological activity', then it becomes clear just how contentious and important the issue can be.

Entwhistle (1978: 32), in emphasising the differences between the social classes in terms of their different cultures and associated linguistic differences, explains the difficulties that working-class children have traditionally had in schooling as being partly due to 'the inability of working-class speech to support academic discourse'. Furthermore, Bernstein (1964: 25), in studying social relationships and how they tend to generate different speech systems (or linguistic codes), argued that the failure of children from working-class origins to profit from formal education was 'crudely related to the control on types of learning induced by a restricted code'. In outlining the difference between what he defines as 'elaborated' and 'restricted' codes in terms of class structures, he states that:

> ... children socialised within middle class and associated strata can be expected to possess both an elaborated and a restricted code whilst children socialised within some sections of the working class strata, particularly the lower working class, can be expected to be limited to a restricted code. As a child progresses through school it becomes critical for him to possess, or at least to be oriented towards, an elaborated code, if he is to succeed.
>
> **(Bernstein 1964: 5)**

There have been a variety of cases whereby parents, including politicians, whilst supporting the principle of comprehensive schools, have sent their own children to private, independent or grammar schools. The reasons behind this apparent contradiction cannot necessarily be ascertained. Whilst it is natural to want the best for one's children, what can be difficult to fathom, is why measures which would enhance children's spoken language skills (such as the insistence on the use of Standard English) cannot be implemented and supported, such that many more can achieve within comprehensive schools. An interesting anecdote relating to the above came during the interview for a magazine article, conducted by Brown (2008) in the 'Sunday Telegraph', of a well known musician to commemorate his 50th birthday. In the interview, the musician, who had been involved during the 80s in many Labour Party causes, said in relation to why he sent his children to private schools, that he didn't want them, '... coming home speaking like Ali G ...'

However, it should be made clear here that the idea of the failure of working-class children being related to linguistic, or cultural deprivation has been challenged by several linguists, including Labov (1972: 201) who, in his studies in the use of black English vernacular of children in urban ghettos, argued that 'the concept of verbal deprivation has no basis in social reality'. Furthermore, Cameron, in her book 'Verbal Hygiene' has argued that:

> 'Non-standard and unconventional uses of language can only be seen as a threat to communication if communication itself is conceived in a way that negates our whole experience of it.'
>
> **(Cameron 1995: 25)**

More recent research, reported by Clark (2009: 1) in the 'Daily Mail' has found that many children from socio-economically disadvantaged backgrounds start school unable to speak or communicate properly as a result of being brought up in environments where there is a lack of communication, and that their speech and language skills are well below children of a similar age.

During the summer of summer of 2008 there was a fiasco relating to the production of the key stage SATS (Standard Attainment Targets) results within schools across England. The fiasco centred around both the late production of many of the results and the many complaints related to the accuracy of the marking. One of the many cases that was highlighted concerned the marking of two key stage 2 English papers for 11 year olds at a school in England. It was reported in newspapers that the primary school head had complained about the marking on the basis that the 2 papers (written by pupil A and pupil B) had been scored equally for sentence structure (5 out of 8 for each) and that pupil B had scored one mark more for composition and effect (9 out of 10 compared with 8 out of 10). Sections of the papers in question were as follows:

Pupil A
Quickly, it became apparent that Pip was a fantastic rider: a complete natural. But it was his love of horses that led to a tragic accident. An accident that would change his life forever. At the age of 7, he was training for…

Pupil B
If he wasent doing enth'ing els heel help his uncle Herry at the funfair during the day. And then hed stoody at nigh…

Although the assessment clearly calls into question how such markers were recruited by the QCA (DfES) to assess the key stage 2 English papers and to what extent they were qualified and trained for the job, it also begs the question as to what extent, and how quickly, pupils who make such errors in their writing assessments are given the opportunity to learn from their mistakes and develop their literacy skills as they progress through compulsory education. Furthermore, on the basis that such errors are commonplace amongst pupils, and always have been, it begs the question as to what extent could they be anticipated and measures put into place to ensure learning through consistent reinforcement of correct spelling, grammar and punctuation across all academic subject areas. Alongside these questions, I also reflect on the extent to which pupils pass through the education system without having their spoken language, in terms of their grammar and pronunciation constantly and consistently corrected where necessary.

At the time of writing (2009), a well rehearsed presentation is going around the schools and colleges of the country highlighting radical changes that are occurring within the 14 – 19 national curriculum, including changes to GCSEs, the introduction of functional skills, the introduction of new foundation, higher and advanced diplomas, an increase in the number and range of apprenticeships, an employment with training option at 16 and the introduction of a Foundation Learning Tier for those learners not ready for a full level 2 qualification. During the video clips within the presentation, school and college managers, teachers and students alike reflect positively on the new qualifications and the range of options available at 14, 16, 17 and 18. What was not reflected on during the presentation however, was how those students studying within the Foundation Learning Tier spoke with non-standard English features (with regards their pronunciation and grammar) as compared with those students aiming for higher level qualifications, whose English tended more towards Standard English (with regards to their pronunciation and grammar). I raised the issue of language during questions at the end of the presentation, and related it to the absence of the speaking of Standard English from the functional skills standards. I left, as I so often do after such meetings wondering if questions I ask will ever be addressed or reflected on, whether or not such questions are ever raised by anyone elsewhere and feeling self conscious that I may be seen at best as eccentric and at worst as a pain in the neck for having raised the subject.

At the time of writing, unions are debating whether or not to boycott SATs in England (they are not held in Wales, Scotland or Northern Ireland). The benefits of such tests to school pupils and the use to which they are put in informing school league tables are questioned in light of increased workloads for teachers and increased stress levels amongst the pupils themselves. Related to the SATS, it has also become a fairly widely held view amongst teachers that measuring is more important than learning. With this, and the above, in mind, I would propose a method of assessment whereby there is less emphasis on measuring, and more on the learning process (i.e. a learning assessment, examples of which, along with a rationale, are given later).

I should say that the situation in schools depicted earlier is clearly not uniform. The focus is on schools in areas where literacy levels amongst its pupils (and often their immediate family) is below a standard expected of their age and where the need for improved speaking skills is therefore greatest.

It should be stated however that in recent years, much money and effort have been invested by the education system in initiatives to support pupils in their literacy. Such initiatives have include the introduction in 1997 of the 'literacy hour' in the primary school curriculum and the widespread deployment of teaching assistants to support pupils with a wide range of special educational needs in primary and secondary schools. Also, even though the principle of encouraging students through praise in order to raise self esteem is one which is well established by teachers, the difficulties involved in motivating students, particularly in the context of teaching in inner-city secondary schools, can not be underestimated.

In schools where efforts have been made to improve the language of its pupils (for example in an Academy school in Manchester, where the pupils are told to use formal language (instead of street slang) with adults within the school at all times, it is regarded as a factor in the school's improved results for achievement of 5 good GCSEs.

However, as stated in the CBI report (2006: 1), '*Working on the three Rs*', which was set up to explore, '… the ways in which literacy… skills are used in the workplace and the shortfalls in these skills that employers experience.':

> Spelling and grammar are important and are widely seen as weak. Correct spelling of everyday words and proper use of basic grammar are important for clarity of expression and fostering a reader's confidence'
>
> **(CBI 2006: 2)**

Furthermore, the report states that, '*The inability to put together a short coherent piece of writing has serious implications for those seeking work or thinking of changing jobs*'. Whilst such experiences and opinions may be commonplace amongst employers, what is not considered or reflected on in the report is why those employers do not set any literacy standard as a prerequisite for employment. If this was done, pressure could be brought to bear on whatever educational establishments the potential employees were at, or at least a dialogue established between employers and such establishments, related to expectations of the literacy levels of potential employees (taking into account however that some may have been statemented as having dyslexia or other learning disorder or disability). Behind each person with low literacy skills however is a cultural system of low expectations which allows many people to leave education and enter the work with those low literacy skills.

This low level of expectations in terms of pupils' literacy standards, which is so apparent in parts of our compulsory education system, transposes (and manifests) itself into our further education system. The whole nature of Key Skills for example does, I believe, act as a compensatory model for those students leaving school with low level literacy skills and yet reflects the low standards and low expectations of the state school system.

In my role as essential skills trainer for a private training company, I provide literacy (communication) and numeracy (application of number) tuition and support for learners who are studying for 'Skills for Life' adult literacy and numeracy qualifications and work-based learning apprenticeship and advanced apprenticeship programmes in the hospitality, retail, care and sport and leisure sectors (alongside tuition and support for the company's staff who need to achieve their level 3 key skills communication and application of number tests). The learners themselves are a mixture of males and females, of all ages (16+ although predominantly in the 16 – 21 age range), from a variety of occupations and from different regions of the country. My experience of teaching literacy to learners in my current job role (and previous job roles within further education) has clearly shown me that there is a correlation between grammar used in spoken English and the grammar used in written English, and that in some cases this is preventing learners from identifying grammatical errors in their own writing and key skills tests, and hence holding them back. Whilst tutoring learners, and facilitating 'On-Line' key skills communication and adult literacy national tests (at levels 1 and 2), I have noticed that learners make reading errors in questions relating to a knowledge of grammar, such as being aware of appropriate verb tense, subject-verb agreement, double negatives and in the use of modal verbs.

These errors may come about as a result of learners not being aware of what grammatical errors are, or when they do, not being able to recognise incorrect (or correct) grammar. Whilst a learner can be taught what grammar is (or what it relates to) and hence what grammatical errors are, it can be more difficult to teach 'correct' or 'Standard English' grammar when it contrasts with learners' spoken English, particularly if that English was not (or rarely) corrected throughout their schooling, and if that is the English they are used to speaking in their home environment

Examples of spoken 'errors' relating to appropriate verb tense include those such as:

'The players come at us' 'The players **came** at us'

'I see him in town yesterday' **'I saw** him in town yesterday'

'He run at me' 'He **ran** at me'

'They give it to him this morning' 'They **gave** it to him this morning'

Examples of spoken 'errors' relating to subject-verb agreement include:

'Was you there last night?' **'Were you ...**

'It weren't really necessary' **'It wasn't** ...

'We done the work earlier' **'We did ...**

Examples of spoken 'errors' relating to double negatives include:

'We haven't got none' **'We haven't got any'**

'I never did nothing' **'I never did anything'**

Examples of spoken 'errors' relating to modal verbs:

'I could of have done it!' **I could have ...**

'Shouldn't they of arrived this morning' **'Shouldn't they have ...**

It is apparent then that written errors that learners make are a reflection on errors that learners make in their spoken English. Bearing in mind that the learners are of both genders, work in a variety of occupations, come from different regions of the country and are of different ages etc, then this, I believe is a reflection at least to a degree on the learners' socio-economic background.

Interestingly, two of the apprenticeship sector skills councils, namely 'People First' (for hospitality) and 'Sports Active' (for sport and leisure) have recently changed the required key skills attainment levels of their apprenticeship programmes, such that learners need now to obtain level one (previously level 2) in communication. Level one is regarded as equivalent to the level required by school children when they have reached the age of eleven, and is therefore a clear indication that standards are being lowered and that allowance is being made for learners' literacy and language deficit.

With regards the Qualifications and Curriculum Authority's 'Key Skills Qualifications Standards and Guidance' (2004) it is stated that with reference to the writing of documents at any level, there should be 'a tolerance level of '... one or two spelling mistakes' and that:

> The same error occurring more than once in a single document counts as a single error. At any level, where a candidate is using punctuation, sentence structures or vocabulary beyond the demands of the standards at that level, errors in their use should not be penalised. Fitness for purpose is an important factor. Several minor errors in a document written for one's own personal use or for limited internal circulation can be considered acceptable...
>
> **(QCA 2004: 29)**

In terms of punctuation, the standards state that at level 1:

> In final work, sentences must be marked correctly by capital letters and full stops or question marks. Where other types of punctuation are used, the candidate should not be penalised for occasional errors, providing meaning is still clear.
>
> **(QCA 2004: 33)**

In other words, the use of the comma and apostrophe are not seen as important at this level. There's a strong likelihood with learners on vocational programmes that they would already have gone through a school system whereby such basics as the correct use of these punctuation marks was not given much (if any) degree of importance. To compensate for this, tutors and assessors need to mentally adjust (consciously or otherwise) by putting in their own punctuation in order to decipher meaning.

Lynne Truss's, 'Eats Shoots and Leaves' illustrates and highlights well the importance of punctuation in everyday contexts and how it can radically change meaning. However, such views relating to the importance of punctuation are criticised on the basis that its rules have exceptions and are not always clear-cut. This may be so. However, there is, I believe, a tendency for people, particularly academics, to focus on the exceptions, and I would argue that in the majority of cases of punctuation errors made by learners, the usage is simply wrong, with the required correction being both necessary and apparent. What can be difficult, is dealing with the lack of importance attached to punctuation by people in general and those in education in particular.

If we consider the fact that some assessors and teachers may not themselves have the literacy skills to identify certain grammatical, spelling and punctuation errors, combined with a broad interpretation that can be given to these standards, particularly in relation to a widely held notion that '... as long as you can still understand the meaning of what's being written, then it's ok ...' adds sustenance to a point of view that the expectations of learners' literacy levels is generally low and that the maintenance of literacy standards are of low importance. This in turn is a contributory factor to the problem of poor literacy levels of many people in Britain.

The effect of regional variation on language use is considered in the adult literacy core curriculum (DfES: 116), in the section for Entry 3 level writing, which states under 'Sentence Focus (Grammar and punctuation)' that 'Adults should be taught to: use correct basic grammar', but to 'understand that in some regional varieties of spoken English the subject and verb do not always agree (e.g. *we was*, *he were*) ...'. It goes on to state however that, '... as written English is a non-regional standard, writers use the same written forms wherever they live'. What is not considered however is how subject-verb agreement relates to socio-economic class, and how a learner's spoken English impacts upon their written English and how such issues can be overcome.

Related to the debate surrounding the use of standard or non-standard English grammar, is the debate concerning the importance, or otherwise, of how words are pronounced. Trudgill (1994) gives examples of a range of accent features including 'TH-FRONTING' in words such as 'thing' and 'thought' (pronounced as 'fing' and 'fought') and 'brother' and 'with' (pronounced as 'bruver' and 'wiv') and explains how they come about as a result of 'f' and 'v' being 'pronounced further forward in the mouth. He also gives the example of how the 't' in words such as 'better' and 'bottle' is being pronounced in a 'new way' as a 'GLOTTAL STOP' which he describes as '... a sound which is produced in the larynx, by momentarily closing the vocal cords.' He also explains the way in which such accent features spread across the country and how they are becoming more common amongst the young. Trudgill (1994) argues that such variations and changes in the way words are pronounced are not undesirable. He backs this up through giving examples and explaining how words such as 'thin', when pronounced as 'fin', would not be confused with a fish's fin due to the context in which the word is used. I take his point although there are examples where the context may not be clear and meaning could be confused, for example with the statement, 'I **f**ought very hard'. However, regardless of context, I believe that what is not made clear is the degree to which non-standard grammar and varying pronunciation features relate to social class and impact upon a learner's reading and writing skills.

In my experience, there is a clear correlation between the use of pronunciation features outlined above and the aforementioned non-standard grammar. That doesn't mean to say that all those who make what I regard as 'grammatical errors' speak with any of the pronunciation variations mentioned above. For example, in some dialects, people may simply say 'you was' instead of 'you were' or use 'come' instead of 'came' (for the past simple of the verb 'to come') and make no other grammatical 'errors' nor speak with any of the pronunciation variations stated. However, I find that the greater the degree of regional variation in grammatical forms, the greater is the tendency towards the use of such pronunciation features, or similar, outlined.

I'm not saying that people from the middle and upper classes don't make 'mistakes' in their spoken grammar or that they don't have their own distinct accent variations which create a 'dialectic mismatch', because they do, it's just that the focus here is specifically on those who don't achieve in education and are, I believe, consequently at a disadvantage when it comes to learning within the education system.

The adult literacy core curriculum and the afore-mentioned national tests in communication, were introduced as part of the government's 'skills for life strategy', launched in 2001, the aim of which is 'to improve the literacy, language and numeracy skills of 1.5m adults in England' by 2007, including young people and adults in low-skilled jobs. However, in spite of much investment, it was reported recently by Smithers (2006) in 'The Guardian' that:

> Up to 16 million adults – nearly half the workforce – are holding down jobs despite having the reading and writing skills expected of children leaving primary school ...
>
> **(Smithers 2006: 1)**

This not only begs the question as to what attention is really being made in many of our schools with regards quite basic literacy and language skills, but also what measures policymakers and OFSTED inspectors are putting in place to ensure all learners develop sufficient literacy and language skills to benefit from, and progress within, their education.

I believe that the attainment of a L1 or L2 test pass is not necessarily evidence in itself of strong numeracy or literacy skills. I say that on the basis that a pass can be achieved with little more than half marks on a multiple choice test. Weak areas in, for example, grammar, punctuation and spelling may still persist, whilst any of the afore-mentioned issues related to spoken English are not considered

Associated and directly linked with issues regarding grammar and pronunciation, are issues related to the reading skills of learners. There were programmes reflecting concerns over the reading skills of children in schools on the TV during the course of 2008, including for example, 'Lost for Words' and 'Dispatches' ('Why our children can't read' and its follow up, 'Last Chance Kids', both on Channel 4). The programmes emphasised the fact that too many children in our schools either can not read, or are reading at a level well below that expected for their age. They highlighted such statistics as:

- 1 in 5 leave primary school at the age of 11 not being able to read and write (properly) to the required standard.

- 118,000 finish primary school every year not being able to read, ¾ of them being white working class and 60% of them being boys
- 11% can't read
- 81% leave school at 16
- 35% have no qualifications and so on.

The programmes have illustrated how the return of, and now increased use of, synthetic phonics (which was until recently not the most dominant method for teaching children how to read) to the curriculum (and hence its increased use) has radically improved the reading skills of children, particularly the weakest 25% or so of schools' pupils. It was argued that for those not in the bottom 25%, there was less dependency on the use of any particular method to assist their reading skills and that they could learn from any one method or range of teaching methods deployed.

In brief, the synthetic phonics system of teaching reading is focused around eliciting the production of the sounds that make up the words and then blending them together to make words i.e. learning the sounds the letters make and linking basic sounds to corresponding words. The system has been shown to be successful in primary schools in London and Scotland. The system was developed by Ruth Miskin, who commented on the fact that children had 'not been taught relentlessly until they can read'.

However, during these programmes, there was no apparent correlation made relating to the fact that many of those who struggled with their reading (along with some of the parents of the school children interviewed) had spoken with non-standard dialects and used a high degree of accent variation i.e. made 'errors' in their grammar and pronunciation, such as those discussed earlier. I am not saying that weak grammar and pronunciation is the cause of poor reading (no more than I am saying that it is the cause of illiteracy or street crime or gang culture etc), but it is surely clear that those who speak with non-standard grammar and a high degree of accent variation are disproportionately represented amongst those said people.

Another recent programme featured an award winning secondary school teacher endeavouring to teach a class of adults how to read. In spite of bust ups and students walking out, i.e. obligatory 'made for reality TV' features, the programme showed the teacher successfully deploying synthetic phonics to develop his learners' reading skills, whilst casting aside the adult literacy core curriculum in the process. However, what in my view appeared to be missing, was again any kind of recognition of the fact that all the learners made 'grammatical errors' and used pronunciation variations such as those outlined earlier, in their spoken English. Consequently, the learners' spoken English was not corrected and no correlation was made between their spoken English and their reading and writing skills.

The importance of the connection between speaking and listening, and reading and writing is clearly illustrated in a radio 4 interview with Sir Jim Rose, who was commissioned by the Department for Children, Schools and Families to carry out an independent review of the primary curriculum, the largest review of its type for 40 years. During the interview, the focus of which was to explore the affects of 'word poverty' on formal learning, it was recognised that a high percentage of children in some areas of the country started school with such poor language skills and such a limited vocabulary, that they weren't able to start reading, and it was stated that 'reading and writing feed off speaking and listening' and that 'if they can't say it, they can't write it.'

It is apparent that a learner's lack of reading skills clearly disadvantages them in their education, and that this disadvantage deepens as they progress through their education and as the gap between them and those who have more competent reading skills gets wider and wider. I believe that not having access to the use of standard grammar and 'correct' pronunciation (and hence sufficient or relevant language) in the school/educational environment further deepens this disadvantage.

To assist in the development of reading skills, pupils need to be given the opportunity to talk and listen more in the classroom. In so doing, they can be given the chance to express ideas and listen to, and learn from, the ideas of others, whilst providing an opportunity to have their grammar and pronunciation corrected where necessary. This would be of particular benefit to children from lower socio-economic groups who, as stated earlier, often begin their schooling with limited language skills compared with those from more middle class backgrounds.

Year upon year it is reported that soon after formal education begins, bright working-class children fall behind in their education, and although there has been a plethora of research and reports highlighting the fact that pupils from deprived areas under-achieve partly as a result of attending under-performing schools, there has been little in the way, accompanying such research, as to how language and literacy can be used as tools for social equality and advancement for those children from deprived areas.

On that basis; bearing in mind the enormous disadvantages caused by language and reading deficiency, and in order to try and compensate for those disadvantages, I would advocate the introduction of elocution lessons for children at as young an age as possible i.e. during the time they are learning to read (which is usually their first year of compulsory schooling). Naturally, this would need to be done delicately, whilst giving a lot of praise. I know in reality that this may not happen, (no matter what arguments are put forward) and that it may be seen as a non starter in principal, even before the issue of logistics, staffing and funding were to be considered. What should happen though is a collective approach amongst policy makers, educationalists and teachers to rigorously correct, as and when necessary, their students' spoken English in terms of their grammar and pronunciation. Many opportunities should be provided for students to talk, within as condusive and relaxed an environment as possible, so that such correction can take place The teaching of synthetic phonics does, I believe, offer an opportunity for this to occur as it involves making sounds and blending them together. Naturally, the greater the intake of students from lower socio-economic groups, the greater will be the degree of error correction necessary. This will also assist in the National Curriculum's aim, which requires youngsters to be competent in Standard English. The degree of correction will naturally depend on each student's background and the level of spoken English that they bring to the class. It could be just a case of tweaking here and there. It is relatively easy to spot and correct grammatical errors, but those relating to pronunciation are not necessarily so easy to pick up on, but nonetheless important. As mentioned earlier there's a tendency for those from lower socio-economic groups in parts of the country to mispronounce the 'th' as '**f**' in words such as 'think' and 'thought' as '**f**ink' and '**f**ought' or as '**v**' in words such as 'with' and 'bother' as 'wi**v**' and 'bo**v**er'; and to not pronounce the 't' or 'tt' that occurs in the middle of a word (e.g. in la**t**er, compu**t**er, solici**t**or or be**tt**er). The mispronunciation of words, combined with incorrect grammar, are factors which lead to a 'dialectic mismatch' between the student and their teacher and therefore puts the student at a distinct disadvantage, a disadvantage which increases as the student progresses through their education. If there is to be any degree of elocution or correction/tweaking of grammar and pronunciation, then it should be done across all academic subject areas. It needs to be instinctive and carried out with some degree of feeling and passion, and understanding of the rationale behind why it should be done.

It is often argued that language can, and should be, adapted to suit its purpose and audience. For example, in an educational setting we should use more formal language, whilst talking with friends in a social environment more informal language is appropriate. That's fine except most children (and adults) who make consistent grammatical errors and mispronounce some of their words, do not, or are not able to switch from one use of language to another simply because they don't know (or are not aware of) the correct grammar to use and the correct pronunciation of certain words. All this leads to them being disadvantaged. It's important to note then that all the examples we are looking at take place in a formal (educational) setting.

Furthermore, I believe that those who speak non-standard English in terms of their grammar and pronunciation are disproportionately represented amongst those who:

- Are unemployed.
- Have low paid jobs.
- Originate from, and stay within, lower socio-economic groups, and form the underclass of society.
- Are involved in gangs and are perpetrators of crime.

- Are victims of gang-related crime and crime generally.
- Have low literacy levels and struggle to read and write.
- Have limited cultural interests.
- Live in socially deprived areas, and find it more difficult to access services.

Effectively, to make Britain literate, you almost have to overturn a history of class society. I do not claim to be a linguist, I just have a real interest in the subject area and some knowledge through subject specialist teaching (literacy and ESOL) courses and from my own reading and research. It's in part about what I want to hear, and what I believe I should be hearing and how it affects me. It's also about how I believe it affects the culture, life chances and prospects of the individuals I hear and see around me. I wonder to what extent policymakers are exposed and affected by, on a daily basis and over a period of time, to the language of lower working class kids on the streets and in their schools, colleges and workplaces.

Education is not neutral with respect to inequalities in society and any consideration of what is involved in counteracting disadvantage should involve consideration of the origins of different groups of students. It has been argued that education favours middle-class students more than working class students on the basis that their system of values and culture more closely identifies with that of the teachers and the educational system they're in. Add to this arguments by Bernstein (1964), National Commission on Education (1993) and Hoggart (1958), concerning the effects of culture, language aspirations and perceptions on working class children in education, then the size of the disadvantage facing them becomes accentuated. Does not the fact that class society, and its effects upon people's education and life chances, continues to exist in spite of whatever government policies are in force and whatever changes are brought about within the education system as a result, mean that in many ways, one system is the concomitant of another (a case in point being the continued failure of working class children when the 'tripartite system of schooling gave way to comprehensivisation)? Furthermore, it can be argued that it exists because it's functional and the education system at all levels (in spite of whatever changes) functions within it, and no political system really has the ability, will, or even necessarily the need to challenge it. By that I mean that class society as it is lends itself towards a capitalist and/or a socialist system.

In brief, a capitalist system for example relies on a lower working class (or underclass), generally less educated and cultured than the rest, to carry out the more menial jobs, or indeed to be unemployed, and to act as the lower strata of society for the above strata. With only so many professional, skilled and well paid jobs around there is I guess a logic to that. A more Socialist system on the other hand has its roots in the working class, and historically oppressed and marginalised sectors of society. These diverse sectors of society have a culture and the language they use to communicate is part of that culture. To try and amend or criticise that language (even though it would potentially benefit them and increase people's chances of a better education and expose them to a wider culture) is seen as an attack on lower socio-economic groups rather than an attack on the injustices that create them, and generally isn't considered. In other words, within the 'class struggle' itself are the roots of its own demise.

So, in effect, one system is the concomitant of the other in as much there has been no clear cut desire or movement within educational departments of political establishments to challenge or improve the spoken language of the working class. Why else then if you were to trawl the towns and cities of Britain, would you hear so many poorly spoken people, disproportionately represented amongst the inner city schools, FE colleges, single mothers on council estates, workers in traditional working class jobs, the service sector in general, the unemployed, and those involved in gang culture and/or street crime, along with their victims. There are of course many successful working class people, but for every sportsman, businessman, pop star or actor who makes it in their career (and who benefits from the erstwhile commercial exploitation of their culture), many more fail to achieve to anywhere like their full potential, caused, in part, by their lack of language and its effect on their academic and cultural development. But you have, I think, got to hear and feel and experience the lack of language and culture on a regular basis, not like it and want to change it.

I would argue that it is not the so-called middle class system of values that are responsible for the failure of working class children (as is sometimes perceived), more that it is the failure by schools and colleges, and policy makers to bring working class children and their associated culture into line with this middle class system of values (at least in terms of language ...) that is more likely to blame for their failure in education, since it is the more middle class children who succeed in education. As Zera and Jupp argue:

> If we are serious about including people with a history of educational failure, people for whom Education is a second language, ethnic minority groups, then we have to reproduce for them some of the things that the middle class take for granted. Sooner or later we will have to recognise the lack of a convincing strategy to combat educational failure. Sooner or later the country will have to make changes to the sacrosanct mainstream so that the norms for one group become the opportunities for all.
>
> **(Zera and Jupp 2000: 138 & 139)**

There seems to be a resistance to this within middle class culture in education based on the notion that one shouldn't be judgemental, undermine or seek to change another class or cultural system of values, whilst at the same time seeing elements of one's own class or culture somehow as a barrier or success of another. This is in part due to a problem that policy makers, managers, educationalists and teachers alike have in education of trying to represent and promulgate a class of people whom they themselves don't identify with. This, combined with the afore-mentioned fact that certain groups have a resistance to education on the basis that they see it as reflecting the values of other social classes, only reinforces the class divide that exists within education and society. Blame, however, doesn't need to be put on middle class values or on working class resistance to education, but neither does a complacent attitude of language use (and its association with class culture) being different but of equal worth, when although very generally speaking, one leads to greater academic success in education and greater levels of attainment in post-16 education and training and greater life chances. Furthermore, I would argue that in looking at the dominant class culture that is represented amongst those who fail in education, ways need to be looked at to change that culture if we consider that in general terms, class society exists as a result of deep rooted historical and social injustices, we must challenge not only the causes of those injustices, but the consequences of the culture produced by those injustices, not consolidate them.

So, from the teacher educators (who speak and use standard English, yet promulgate the use of non-standard English through not correcting it sufficiently), to the indifferent speakers of standard English to the low skilled worker and unemployed people (who use non-standard English), many of those in potential positions of influence are collectively responsible for the low level of expectations in terms of literacy standards of many people in this country and the concomitant low literacy levels of those people.

Pupils should not only be able to work comfortably at a reasonable level of literacy long before they leave secondary school, the importance of being literate to this degree should be installed into them long before they leave secondary school. The fact that in my job role, I observe on a daily basis that many of the learners I work with are not able to speak (or write) in standard English, I believe is a fairly clear sign that like it or not, the argument has been lost.

One of the reasons so many people have difficulties in spelling, punctuation and grammar is because they have not had basic rules consistently reinforced throughout their schooling. This lack of consistency then continues through, as stated earlier, into further education. Look around any college of further education and listen to how many of the full time learners speak among themselves. If they've recently been through 11 years of education without having their grammar or pronunciation consistently corrected (and all that that entails relating to their literacy and communication skills), then it's very unlikely they'll respond to much of a degree now, or be encouraged to reflect upon and adapt their spoken English (again with all that that entails relating to their literacy and communication skills). Somehow it just isn't seen as important, and people can even be at best indifferent, and at worst scornful, of attempts to even raise the issue. As mentioned earlier, it's not a case of wanting learners to 'talk posh' amongst themselves, it's about learners, within an educational or professional environment, being able to utilise Standard English, whether through speaking or writing (or both) for their own advantage, and hence not being disadvantaged.

I believe that language use is determined by one's socio-economic status or social group (as well as age and gender), and the context in which the language is used. However, I also believe that in order for literacy to be a tool for providing greater equality of opportunity for some social groups, then the effects of non-standard English use on the educational achievements of those social groups needs to be given greater consideration. Promoting the principal of Equality of Opportunity isn't enough when what is required for the provision of equality of opportunity is not understood or provided for. The results of this lack of understanding are all too apparent when we see the consequences for the many people who are left behind.

Although there has been a plethora of research and reports highlighting the fact that pupils from deprived areas under-achieve partly as a result of attending under-performing schools, there has been little in the way, accompanying such research, as to how language and literacy can be used as tools for social equality and advancement for those children from deprived areas.

Returning then to the argument as to whether or not the use of standard English should be enforced in schools, it is clear from listening to many of the children within our inner-city schools and students within FE colleges, that the argument in favour of standard English has been lost.

What I perceive of as poor or incorrect grammar and pronunciation is passed on from generation to generation within the home environment. Pupils entering the education system using non-standard English leave it several years later (whether it be school, FE college or training provider) having rarely (if at all) had their use of non-standard spoken English challenged or corrected in circumstances where it should have been , a factor which contributes significantly to the cycle of failure that many users of non-standard English enter.

A serious debate needs to be started over the issue of spoken English and literacy within schools and post-16 education providers. If literacy standards do not increase substantially, then any ideas expressed have failed, whether or not they were ever considered in the first place, as indeed were any previous initiatives.

In conclusion, I am advocating the following:

- Elocution and/or constant correction of grammar and pronunciation, beginning in primary school and continuing through secondary and post-16 education.

- Greater use of talking and listening activities in primary schools in order to develop vocabulary, speaking skills and confidence I expressing ideas.

- Constant correction of spelling, punctuation and grammar (appropriate to pupils' levels) within English classes during primary school, across the curriculum throughout secondary education and within all academic and vocational areas in post-16 education. The latter point will in turn help to develop parity of esteem between the academic and vocational areas, post-16.
- The development and introduction of learning assessments to replace SATS within primary and secondary schools, and to replace current literacy initial and diagnostic assessments within post-16 institutions.
- Connected with the above points, all those involved directly in education to have higher expectations of learners' literacy levels.

The main focus of this is book isn't so much about resources for developing literacy skills, as there is an abundance of good resources available from many quarters, it's more about setting a framework for the potential development of language and literacy skills. Such a framework includes, in the context of educational settings, greater awareness of the importance spoken language (grammar and pronunciation) and its association with the development of learners' literacy skills, and all that entails in terms of providing a greater access to curricula and a wider culture, and hence better life chances. It does however contain a literacy learning assessment (referred to earlier), along with a rationale for its use, and a range of related resources.

Rationale behind the Literacy Learning Assessments and literacy resources

Like the numeracy learning assessment, the literacy learning assessments focus on areas of difficulty that many learners face, and give the learner (facilitated by a tutor) the opportunity to dovetail into areas of required learning through the assessment and feedback process. Also (again like the numeracy learning assessment) it replaces the need for initial and diagnostic assessments (where no learning takes place) with an integrated practical learning assessment (where learning can take place) which is routed in the context of having high expectations of all learners. The learning assessments are offered at 2 levels, a judgement being needed by a tutor as to which one would be more appropriate for any given learner. They allow tutors to develop skills in providing effective and focused feedback to learners and in so doing, provide learning opportunities for them. Leading on from the feedback, the learning assessments can be used and developed as learning resources. With current paper-based and computer-based initial and diagnostic assessments, there is no real involvement in the learning process by the tutor, the assessment being manually (or automatically) marked, followed by a level being administered, which is a process requiring little skill. Although a marking scheme and time limit for the assessment are suggested, it can be regarded as flexible, as indeed can the makeup and/or weighting of the questions and assignment of a level to a given mark. On the one hand a need for the assignation of a level can be required for purposes of differentiation between learners, on the other, the focus of the learning assessments, it should be remembered, should be on providing the opportunity to learn. Rather than an area of difficulty being diagnosed as 'spelling', a tutor may be able to determine more specifically from the 'dictated sentences' and 'free writing' parts of the literacy learning assessments the types or patterns of spelling error made by the learner and offer solutions through reinforcing of spelling rules, identifying spelling patterns and providing the opportunity for repetition of those patterns. These areas of difficulty may include:

- Understanding of spelling rules in words such as 'families' ('y' à 'ies' when forming plurals) and 'receive' ('e' before 'i' after a 'c').
- Misuse of homophones (same sounding words such as there/their; here/hear; too/to; your/you're etc).
- Omission of letters such as the first 'e' in different (and difference), the 'c' in 'excellent' or the 'r' in surprise, as they are often not pronounced.
- Failing to omit the 'e' when adding the 'ing' suffix to a verb e.g. 'write' to 'writing' or 'take' to 'taking' etc

- Doubling of the consonant when adding a suffix to a short (or 1 syllable) verb e.g. 'run' to 'running'; 'let' to letting 'plan' to 'planned' etc.

The grammar exercises enable the learner to focus on some of the most common everyday spoken grammatical errors which can be reflected in written English. These errors include the use of double negatives, and 'was' for 'were', 'done' for 'did' and 'come' for 'came' in past tenses. In addition, the literacy learning assessment assesses a wide range of literacy skills (including 'reading for understanding' and 'free writing') whilst allowing the learner to utilise a range of learning styles. In marking and providing feedback to the learner, experience can be gained in identifying and correcting types of spelling, punctuation and grammatical errors made by learners (and in so doing, address an action point frequently raised in external verification key skills reports and issues addressed in the aforementioned, 'Working on the 3 Rs').

The literacy learning assessments focus on developing everyday literacy skills and (as with the numeracy learning assessment), is contextualised and gives learners the opportunity to learn from the assessment itself, including from their own mistakes.

The literacy learning assessments consist of the following 4 areas:

- Spelling (including homophones)
- Grammar
- Reading for understanding (including vocabulary in context,
- punctuation, comprehension and main purpose of text)
- Free writing

Although it's a situation I come across frequently, it rarely ceases to surprise me when I'm asked questions such as, 'What's a verb?' or 'What's a noun?' or 'What's an adjective?' It surprises me because it appears that schooling has in many cases not embedded such knowledge into its pupils sufficiently in spite of the fact that an understanding of such terms can aid grammar, punctuation and spelling and in spite of the fact that such questions can be explained to, and/or elicited from a learner within a matter of minutes through the use of sentences such as the following:

"*The young man drove quickly down the bumpy road*."

With regards to the free writing exercise, one of the areas of difficulty that learners face is the ability to write in complete sentences. A typical error that learners make for example is to use commas instead of full stops at the end of sentences. Exercises such as 'Full Stops and Capital Letters', which focus on where sentences end, can be used to overcome this issue, along with everyday reading of a range of suitable texts, whilst adapting to the punctuation appropriately, and further free writing practice.

Another issue facing learners is the ability to develop complex sentences from simple or compound ones through the use of conjunctions such as when, because, if, whenever, whilst etc. Such conjunctions, when used, turn sentences into complex ones through the formation of a subordinate clause (which does not make sense on its own) accompanying a main clause (which does make sense on its own). For example:

The minibus arrived late because it was delayed by the traffic.

Here, '*The minibus arrived late*' is the main clause, as it can stand on its own and make sense, whilst '*because it was delayed by traffic*' is the subordinate clause, as it does not make sense on its own. To assist in addressing this issue, exercises to locate and highlight simple, compound and complex sentences within a range of text, including those within the dictated sentences, can be carried, out as well as exercises choosing the appropriate conjunction to join two simple sentences, and indicating the main and subordinate clauses. In addition, learners should be encouraged, and given the opportunity, to use complex sentences (along with simple and compound ones) within the context of free writing exercises.

Although the focus of any particular exercise may be on one main aspect of literacy, such as spelling, grammar, reading for overall understanding, scanning for particular information, developing vocabulary or punctuation etc, where possible, other aspects of literacy can be highlighted. Naturally, both within, and outside of, the educational setting, learners should be encouraged to read and engage with written material, be it books, newspapers or magazines) as much as possible. Within the context of the above, the reading of specific, relevant and engaging articles can lend itself to exercises which highlight the use of correct spelling, punctuation and grammar within the text. Such articles can also be used to develop learners' knowledge of unfamiliar vocabulary and phrases or expressions (relating to, for example, specific technical or scientific language which the learners may not be familiar with) in preparation for discussion based around the whole article.

In conclusion, I believe that the facilitation of learning assessments would be an effective way to both develop learners' literacy skills and to support tutors and/or vocational coaches in supporting their learners. Leading on from the learning assessment, a tutor should be able to deliver learning relating to spelling, punctuation, grammar, vocabulary, sentence structure and understanding of text etc using a range of resources.

L1 Learning Assessment (Literacy)

Name: ______________________ **Date:** __________

The purpose of the assessment is to check any weak areas you may have, but more importantly to give you the chance to learn from it, and to develop everyday literacy skills. At the end of the assessment you can take away a copy of your paper together with an answer sheet to learn from.
Time allowed for the assessment: 30 minutes

Mark: ___ / 40 Level: ___

Spelling (12)

Six sentences will be dictated to you by your tutor or vocational coach:

1. ______________________
2. ______________________
3. ______________________
4. ______________________
5. ______________________
6. ______________________

Grammar Exercise (8)

The following conversation between 2 people (A and B) contains some of the most common grammatical errors made in everyday spoken English. There are 8 errors in total, and they are underlined. Place the correct word above.
e.g. 'I done' is incorrect. It should be 'I did'.

A 'Have you done any courses here before?'

B 'Yes, I did a sports therapy course here last year.'

A 'I thought I'd seen you here before. Weren't you a part of that group of students what used the gym lunchtimes?'

B 'That's right. I see you in there sometimes didn't I?'

A 'Yes. What was the sports therapy course like?'

B 'It was really good,'

A 'Did you have an induction for that course too?'

B 'Yes, it was different from this though. I remember we was split up into small groups and had to introduce each other to the whole class. I thought we would have done it in this class too.'

A 'Was that a bit nerve racking?'

B 'It weren't really nerve racking, although some of the students didn't have nothing to say so run off before it was their turn to speak. Was you here yesterday afternoon when we done that ice breaking exercise?'

A 'No I missed it.

Reading for understanding (14)

Read the passage below, and then answer the questions following:

Healthy Eating

Jamie Oliver's grand plan to convert the nation's schools to healthy eating habits got off to a flying start last night at the 'Make Britain Healthier' awards ceremony. Everyone agreed that the ceremony had been a success, and many people were eager to meet Oliver after the show, even if it was just for a brief moment, to ask the celebrity chef for his autograph.

The principal aim of his campaign is to persuade schools to provide meals that are balanced and healthy in order to do this, schools must ensure that their meals contain sufficient amounts of protein carbohydrates (including fibre) and fats, as well as a balance of vitamins and minerals. To achieve this, Oliver has suggested that a wide variety of menus are offered and that the ingredients used in the meals are fresh (i.e non-processed).

Although many say that his plans are good, others have questioned the cost of the plans and asked why children can't be allowed to decide for themselves what to eat. Nevertheless, studies have shown that children's behaviour does improve the healthier their diet becomes, and that if the meals are budgeted for correctly, the amount of money spent by schools on its dinners shouldn't rise.

Q. Match each of the following words below, with a word from the list that is similar in meaning:

enough - ____________	principal - ____________
rise - ____________	eager - ____________
fresh - ____________	balanced - ____________

sufficient, mainly, apparently, short, keen, expensive, decrease, encouraged, evenly distributed, non-processed, exterior, increase, persuaded

Q. List 4 things that a balanced diet should contain:

____

Q. What was the name of the 'Awards Ceremony' in the above article?

____

Q. Give one argument in favour of Jamie Oliver's plan:

____

Q. Give one argument against Jamie Oliver's plan:

____

Q. Write down one adjective used in the above passage.

____

Q. Why does the word 'Oliver' have a capital letter?

____

Q. There is a comma missing from the text. Place it in the correct position in the text.

Q. There is a full stop (followed by a capital letter) missing from the text. Place them in the correct position in the text.

Write 3 short sentences about your own diet (6):

Notes for tutor/vocational coach

Dictate six of the following sentences to the learner:

1. My friend got off the bus and walked to the centre of town.
2. The office managers were surprised to meet their targets in February.
3. She received an excellent prize for her dancing.
4. It doesn't matter too much if your planning application fails.
5. There will always be more chances here to exercise.
6. Please remember to come here earlier on Wednesday.
7. There were different families there yesterday.
8. We weren't allowed through the gates.
9. They went to the library to carry out some research.
10. The warm weather in February was quite unusual.

During the five minutes reading time, learners can be told or reminded of such things as:

- Remember to start each sentence with a capital letter and end it with a full stop (or question mark if it is a question).
- Capital letters should be used for I, days of the week, months of the year, place names, addresses, titles etc.
- For the grammar exercise, search for the verbs that look or sound wrong. If necessary, briefly outline the difference between a verb, noun and an adjective.

Marking

An answer sheet will be provided. In the spelling exercise, two marks should be given for a correct sentence, and one mark if there is one mistake in the sentence. In the free writing exercise, two marks should be given for a correct sentence (i.e. with correct spelling, punctuation and grammar). If there are one or two errors in the sentence, then one mark should be given. If there are more than 2 errors, then no marks should be given. One mark can be given for legibility of the learner's writing.

After the assessment is marked, brief feedback (or as much feedback as the assessor/recruiter feels comfortable with) can be given to the learner along with the answers. The learner then has the option of checking (and hence learning from) their assessment.

L2 Learning Assessment (Literacy)

Name: ______________________ **Date:** ____________

The purpose of the assessment is to check any weak areas you may have, but more importantly to give you the chance to learn from it, and to develop everyday literacy skills. At the end of the assessment you can take away a copy of your paper together with an answer sheet to learn from.
Time allowed for the assessment: 30 minutes

Mark: ___/40 Level: ___

Spelling (12)

Six sentences will be dictated to you by your tutor or vocational coach:

1. ______________________
2. ______________________
3. ______________________
4. ______________________
5. ______________________
6. ______________________

Grammar Exercise (7)

The following conversation between 2 people (A and B) contains some of the most common grammatical errors made in everyday spoken English. There are 8 errors in total. Underline each error and place the correct word above.

A 'Have you done any courses here before?'

B 'Yes, I done a sports therapy course here last year.'

A 'I thought I'd seen you here before. Weren't you a part of that group of students which used the gym lunchtimes?'

B 'That's right. I see you in there sometimes didn't I?'

A 'Yes. What was the sports therapy course like?'

B 'It was really good,'

A 'Did you have an induction for that course too?'

B 'Yes, it was different from this though. I remember we were split up into small groups and had to introduce each other to the whole class. I thought we would of done it in this class too.'

A 'Was that a bit nerve racking?'

B 'It wasn't really nerve racking, although some of the students ran off before it was their turn to speak. Were you here yesterday afternoon when we did that ice breaking exercise?'

A 'No I missed it. We came out of the library at about 2 o'clock, and by the time we got to the class it had finished. They give us some stuff to look at though, so I've got that.'

B 'Could you borrow me your notes later so I could photocopy them?'

A 'O.K. but will you call me when you've finished with them?'

B 'Sure, but I haven't got no credit left on my phone.'

A 'It don't matter, I'll collect them when I see you next

Reading for understanding (15)

Read the passage below and then answer the following questions:

© Mark Bracey

Bronte Country

Welcome to Bronte Country, an area which spans the West Yorkshire and East Lancashire Pennines in the North of England. A windswept land of heather and wild moors, it is hardly surprising that this region became the inspiration for the classic works of the Bronte sisters, Charlotte, Emily and Anne.

Bronte Country consists of the Pennine hills immediately to the west of (but also including) the cities of Bradford and Leeds in West Yorkshire. The geology in Bronte Country is predominantly dark sandstone, which gives the scenery a feeling of bleakness it is no surprise then, that this landscape fuelled the imagination of the Bronte sisters in writing their classic novels including "Wuthering Heights" and "Jane Eyre".

Most of the Bronte locations lie within easy reach of the village of Haworth, where the Bronte family lived at the Haworth parsonage (now the world famous Bronte Parsonage Museum), and where they wrote most of their famous works (including "Wuthering Heights" and "Jane Eyre" etc). Other Bronte related attractions in the heart of Bronte Country include the Bronte Birthplace in Thornton on the outskirts of Bradford (where Charlotte, Emily and Anne were born while their father was parson at Thornton church), and Ponden Hall near Haworth ("Thrushcross Grange" in "Wuthering Heights") and Oakwell Hall in Kirklees.

Other famous people associated with The Bronte Country include the playwright J.B. Priestley, the composer Delius, the novelist John Braine and the artist David Hockney, all of whom (like the Bronte sisters themselves) were born within the 40district of the city of Bradford, and the poet Ted Hughes, who was born near Hebden Bridge.

Do you want to find out more. If you wish to access a full list of places to visit and practical information about Bronte Country, then please take a look at our list of books and other products about the Brontes (and Bronte Country). Alternatively, you can find more information on our website (www.bronte-country.com), including links to accommodation and where to eat etc.

Q. Match each of the following words below, with a word from the list that is similar in meaning:

scenery - ____________________ outskirts - ____________________

novelist - ____________________ predominantly - ____________________

spans - ____________________ bleakness - ____________________

interior, mainly, apparently, landscape, excellent, desolation, secondary, scenic,writer, painter, exterior, crosses, avoids, periphery, picturesque

Q. Where were the Bronte sisters born?

____

Q. Where was 'Jane Eyre' written?

____

Q. What name was given to Ponden Hall in Wuthering Heights?

____

Q. Apart from the Bronte sisters, name two other writers associated with Bronte country:

____

Q. Why do the words 'Wuthering Heights' contain capital letters?

____

Q. There is a question mark missing from the text. Place it in the correct position in the text.

Q. There is a full stop (followed by a capital letter) missing from the text. Place them in the correct position in the text.

Q. The purpose of the image is to:

A) Inform the reader of the attractions of Bronte country.
B) Show the reader where the Pennine hills are located.
C) Give the reader an impression of Bronte country.
D) Show the reader the location of the village of Howarth.

Q. What is the main purpose of the article?

A) To inform the reader of the attractions of Bronte country.
B) To inform the reader where the Bronte sisters were born.
C) To inform the reader about the world famous Bronte Parsonage Museum.
D) To inform the reader of the geology of the landscape.

Free writing (6)

Write 50 – 60 words about a place you have visited recently, **or** about what you did in a previous job role:

Notes for tutor/vocational coach

Dictate six of the following sentences to the learner:

1. I thought it wouldn't be necessary to liaise with my manager.
2. The advertisement received its first endorsement yesterday.
3. To become a professional, you need to have more than just the occasional practice session.
4. The atmosphere in my new accommodation wasn't great.
5. He said, 'We should have practised regularly.'
6. The children's bicycles had their first maintenance check yesterday.
7. The headmaster's secretary welcomed the new Health Commissioner.
8. He told everyone that he would make a significant announcement later in the day.
9. It appears that they are still fighting for independence or a separate homeland.
10. The privileged few were given a particularly hard time.

During the five minutes reading time, learners can be told or reminded of such things as:

- Remember to start each sentence with a capital letter and end it with a full stop (or question mark if it is a question).
- Capital letters should be used for I, days of the week, months of the year, place names, addresses, titles etc.
- For the grammar exercise, search for the verbs that look or sound wrong. If necessary, briefly outline the difference between a verb, noun and an adjective.

Marking

An answer sheet will be provided. In the spelling exercise, two marks should be given for a correct sentence, and one mark if there is one mistake in the sentence. In the free writing exercise, two marks should be given for a correct sentence (i.e. with correct spelling, punctuation and grammar). If there are one or two errors in the sentence, then one mark should be given. If there are more than 2 errors, then no marks should be given. One mark can be given for legibility of the learner's writing.

After the assessment is marked, brief feedback (or as much feedback as the assessor/recruiter feels comfortable with) can be given to the learner along with the answers. The learner then has the option of checking (and hence learning from) their assessment.

Answers to L1 literacy learning assessment

Grammar (8)

A 'Have you done any courses here before?'

B 'Yes, I did a sports therapy course here last year.'

A 'I thought I'd seen you here before. Weren't you a part of that group of students **which** (or **that** or **who**) used the gym lunchtimes?'

B 'That's right. I **saw** you in there sometimes didn't I?'

A 'Yes. What was the sports therapy course like?'

B 'It was really good,'

A 'Did you have an induction for that course too?'

B 'Yes, it was different from this though. I remember we **were** split up into small groups and had to introduce each other to the whole class. I thought we would have done it in this class too.'

A 'Was that a bit nerve racking?'

B 'It **wasn't** really nerve racking, although some of the students didn't have **anything** to say so **ran** off before it was their turn to speak. **Were** you here yesterday afternoon when we **did** that ice breaking exercise?'

A 'No I missed it.

Reading for understanding (14)

Q. Match each of the following words below, with a word from the list that is similar in meaning:

enough - **sufficient**

rise - **increase**

fresh - **non-processed**

principal - **main**

eager - **keen**

balanced – **evenly distributed**

Q. List 4 things that a balanced diet should contain:
Four from; proteins, carbohydrates, fats, vitamins and minerals.

Q. What was the name of the 'Awards Ceremony' in the above article?
'Make Britain Healthier'

Give one argument in favour of Jamie Oliver's plan:
It could improve children's behaviour and/or health or children's school dinners would be healthier or similar answer.

Q. Give one argument against Jamie Oliver's plan:
Children should be allowed to decide for themselves or there could be an increase in costs if school dinners are made healthier or similar answer.

Q. Write down one adjective used in the above passage.
One of grand, healthy, eager, brief, principal, wide, fresh, good

Q. Why does the word 'Oliver' have a capital letter?
Because it is a person's name.

Q. There is a comma missing from the text. Place it in the correct position in the text:
...sufficient amounts of protein**,** carbohydrates (including fibre) and fats, ...

Q. There is a full stop (followed by a capital letter) missing from the text. Place them in the correct position in the text:
...to provide meals that are balanced and healthy**. I**n order to do this, schools must ...

Answers to L2 literacy learning assessment

Grammar (7)

A 'Have you done any courses here before?'

B 'Yes, I **did** a sports therapy course here last year.'

A 'I thought I'd seen you here before. Weren't you a part of that group of students which used the gym lunchtimes?'

B 'That's right. I **saw** you in there sometimes didn't I?'

A 'Yes. What was the sports therapy course like?'

B 'It was really good,'

A 'Did you have an induction for that course too?'

B 'Yes, it was different from this though. I remember we were split up into small groups and had to introduce each other to the whole class. I thought we would **have** done it in this class too.'

A 'Was that a bit nerve racking?'

B 'It wasn't really nerve racking, although some of the students ran off before it was their turn to speak. Were you here yesterday afternoon when we did that ice breaking exercise?'

A 'No I missed it. We came out of the library at about 2 o'clock, and by the time we got to the class it had finished. They **gave** us some stuff to look at though, so I've got that.'

B 'Could you **lend** me your notes later so I could photocopy them?'

A 'O.K. but will you call me when you've finished with them?'

B 'Sure, but I haven't got **any** credit left on my phone.'

A 'It **doesn't** matter, I'll collect them when I see you next

Reading for understanding (15)

Q. Match each of the following words below, with a word from the list that is similar in meaning:

scenery - **landscape**
outskirts - **periphery**
novelist - **writer**
predominantly - **mainly**
spans - **crosses**
bleakness - **desolation**

Q. Where were the Bronte sisters born? **Thornton** or **Bradford**

Q. Where was 'Jane Eyre' written? **The Howarth parsonage**

Q. What name was given to Ponden Hall in Wuthering Heights? **Thorncrush Grange**

Q. Apart from the Bronte sisters, name two other writers associated with Bronte country: Any two from **J B Priestly, John Braine and Ted Hughes**

Q. Why do the words 'Wuthering Heights' contain capital letters? **Because it's the name (or title) of a book** or **because it's a place name**

Q. There is a question mark missing from the text. Place it in the correct position in the text.
Do you want to find out more**?**

Q. There is a full stop (followed by a capital letter) missing from the text. Place them in the correct position in the text.
Bronte Country consists of the Pennine hills immediately to the west of (but also including) the cities of Bradford and Leeds in West Yorkshire. The geology in Bronte Country is predominantly dark sandstone, which gives the scenery a feeling of bleakness. It is no surprise then, that this landscape fuelled the imagination of the Bronte sisters in writing their classic novels including "Wuthering Heights" and "Jane Eyre".

Q. The purpose of the image is to:
A) Inform the reader of the attractions of Bronte country.
B) Show the reader where the Pennine hills are located.
C) Give the reader an impression of Bronte country.
D) Show the reader the location of the village of Howarth.

Q. What is the main purpose of the article?

A) To inform the reader of the attractions of Bronte country.

B) To inform the reader where the Bronte sisters were born.

C) To inform the reader about the world famous Bronte Parsonage Museum.

D) To inform the reader of the geology of the landscape.

Spelling

Some spelling rules

Before trying the following exercises, you should be aware of the following spelling rules:

i and e
Put i before e, except after c, when the sound rhymes with bee.
Examples:

> piece, thief, belief, believe, hygiene, brief, priest, shield, relief, niece, pier, chief, ceiling, receive, receipt, deceive, conceive

However, there are some exceptions e.g. weird and seize

Also, be aware of words where e comes before i when the sound doesn't rhyme with bee e.g. height, weight, leisure, their

Making plural from nouns ending in y
If the letter immediately before the y is a consonant, change the y into i and add –es.
Examples:

> Penny – pennies lorry - lorries industry – industries company – companies

If the letter immediately before the y is a vowel (a, e, i, o u) simply add s
Examples:

> Valley – valleys monkey – monkeys turkey – turkeys

Try remembering the spelling of the following commonly misspelled words. For each word, look at it, cover it, say it, write it out, and then check the spelling: careful, carefully, usual, usually, peaceful, peacefully, sudden, suddenly, occasion, occasional, occasionally, knife, knives, leaf, leaves, shelf, shelves, wife, wives, church, churches, brush, brushes, address, addresses, business, businesses, write, writing, make, making, notice, noticing, excite, exciting, (age, ageing), exercise, carry, carrying, carried, hurry, hurrying, hurried, shop, shopping, travel, travelling, trip, tripped, pass, passed, possess, possessed, necessary, separate, vegetable, different, difference, reference, interest, interesting, computer, mechanic, excellent, always, advertisement, professional, attached, assistant, earlier, surprise, foreign, responsible, responsibilities, Wednesday, February, tomorrow, through, necessary, beautiful, restaurant, early, earlier, science, argue, argument

Punctuation

Read the following information and try the punctuation exercise.

Capital letters are used at the beginning of a sentence, for days of the week (e.g. **W**ednesday) and months of the year (e.g. **F**ebruary), for the word **I**, for proper nouns (place names, people's names and names of countries, mountains and rivers), for addresses, for names of products and brand names (e.g. **W**alkers, **N**ike etc.), for names of festivals (e.g. **C**hristmas, **R**amadan etc), for names of nationalities (e.g. **E**nglish, **C**hinese etc) and for titles (e.g. **M**rs, **D**r etc).

Full stops (.) are placed at the end of sentences**.**

A **question mark (?)** is placed at the end of a sentence which asks a question.
e.g. How do you apply for a passport**?** Do you like sugar**?** Are you alright**?**
However, it is not placed after a statement e.g. How to apply**.**

Exclamation marks (!) are used at the end of a statement showing surprise or shock, or at the end of an order, exclamation or cry e.g. Don't look**!** I don't believe it**!**
The meaning of a sentence can be altered by changing the punctuation mark at the end. For example:

They drove on the motorway. – Statement
They drove on the motorway? – Question
They drove on the motorway! – Exclamation (showing surprise or shock)

Commas (,) are used to mark a pause in a sentence, divide items in a list and to separate part of a sentence which gives information but is not vital to make sense. For example:

I don't like jogging**,** but I enjoy swimming.
We need carrots**,** eggs**,** a couple of loaves of bread**,** mushrooms and carrots.
Next month**,** after we've finished our course**,** we'll start our Christmas shopping.

Apostrophes (')
An omissive **apostrophe** is used to replace a missing letter (or letters) when two words are joined together. For example:

I **do not** know where they are = I **don't** know where they are
We have got six months left = **We've** got six months left

Possessive **apostrophes** are used to indicate that something belongs to someone or something. For example:

The boy's computer = The computer of the boy
The children's books = The books of the children
The lady's coat = The coat of the lady
Ladies' fashions = Fashions of the ladies
The boys' teams = The teams of the boys
In next week's episode = In the episode of next week

L1 Sentence examples

Read the following sentences, then practise writing them:

1. My friend got off the bus and walked to the centre of town.
2. The office managers were surprised to meet their targets.
3. She received an excellent prize for her dancing.
4. It doesn't matter too much if your planning application fails.
5. There will always be more chances here to exercise.
6. Please remember to come here earlier on Wednesday.
7. There were different families there yesterday.
8. We weren't allowed through the gates.
9. He wrote everything down carefully.
10. They went to the library to carry out some research.
11. The warm weather in February was quite unusual.
12. He was hoping to wear the suit that had been designed especially for him.
13. They would only go to the fair if they could go on their favourite rides.
14. The lorries drove quickly down the motorway.
15. She preferred writing at night, when the house was quiet.
16. They had to count their pennies before deciding to go on holiday.
17. Although she was quite old, her eyesight was still good.
18. We listened to the radio all day, but unfortunately our song wasn't played.
19. You need to be careful whilst driving on the right hand side of the road.
20. It was a suitable occasion to celebrate the people's success.
21. The children's books were stacked on the shelves.
22. Weren't you happy with the arrangements at the theatre?

From the above sentences, write down:

2 nouns ____________ ____________

2 adjectives ____________ ____________

2 verbs ____________ ____________

2 adverbs ____________ ____________

Level 1 Literacy Exercise

Read the following passage and make any corrections. There are nine errors to be found.

The managers was surprised to here about the theft. They were told that the thieves had broken into the hotel and stolen there keys. They recieved the news quite late at night. They were told that the thieves had been give to many opportunities to break in.

Have you ever had something stolen.
If your'e planing to make your house more secure, you should do so instantaneously.

L2 Sentence examples

Read the following sentences, then practise writing them:

1. I thought it wouldn't be necessary to liaise with my manager.
2. The advertisement received its first endorsement yesterday.
3. To become a professional, you need to have more than just the occasional practice session.
4. The atmosphere in my new accommodation wasn't great.
5. He said, 'We should have practised regularly.'
6. The children's bicycles had their first maintenance check yesterday.
7. The headmaster's secretary welcomed the new Health Commissioner.
8. He told everyone that he would make a significant announcement later in the day.
9. It appears that they are still fighting for independence or a separate homeland.
10. The privileged few were given a particularly hard time.
11. The Government is clearly struggling in this current recession.
12. The effects of climate change are becoming clearly visible.

13. 'His frenzy was armour for his fear', cried the poet.
14. Scientists are currently debating the degree to which climate change is affecting our environment.
15. Contingency plans were drawn up by the regional executive.
16. The train pulled away unexpectedly, while its international passengers slept.
17. The thermometer showed a rapid rise in temperature.
18. As a result of accumulating debts, he felt obliged to sell his collection of sports cars.
19. The more expensive items in her collection included jewellery, some antique furniture and a Persian rug.
20. The ambassador's residence was well furnished.

Capital Letters and Full Stops

Read the sentences below and place full stops and capital letters where they are needed:

1. i went to brighton last week and i'll go there again tomorrow
2. my friend likes to keep fit he eats healthily and goes swimming most days of the week
3. she took longer than expected to reach the border, because the coach kept stopping
4. harry and steve are flying to berlin in october they'll stay there for about a week, then travel across to britain
5. george felt unwell during the conference, so left before the end

6 i had bacon, eggs tomatoes, beans and mushrooms for breakfast, so for lunch i'll probably just have a tuna sandwich

7 he called the surgery to arrange a telephone appointment with one of the doctors dr john then called him sometime in the afternoon

8 there were lots of people at the party last night most of them were new to the organisation

9 they didn't really want to stay at the sheraton hotel, but at the end of the day they didn't really have much of a choice

10 there were twenty five students in the classroom, all of whom were waiting to do their assessment

11 for lunch we had fishcakes, rice and vegetables then for dessert we had bread and butter pudding with custard

12 i'll never forget that adventure in lake Malawi it's hard to believe that we were stuck in the mud when the flash storm started

Apostrophes (to show belonging)

Place apostrophes in the correct position in the following sentences:

1. The assessors read through the learners portfolio.
2. The verifiers observed the assessors all afternoon.
3. I read the stories in last weeks newspapers.
4. He ran his familys business like anyone elses business.
5. My childrens ages are six and seven.
6. He was the peoples choice.
7. The mens room is just around the corner.
8. The dogs collar is red. It is wagging its tail.
9. He read his brothers book with great enthusiasm
10. She receives her paycheques on a regular basis.

Look at these 4 sentences, then choose the correct answer below:

1. !!!"***… womens …,,,!"**
2. "***,,,,.. peoples --!!!!
3. ""!!::::: mens __---!1!1!!
4. $$£^^^** childrens ""!!!! ---

A) The apostrophe goes after the s in all of the above (s').
B) There is not enough information given to say where the apostrophe should go.
C) The apostrophe goes before the s in each of the above ('s).
D) There is no apostrophe in any of the above.

Grammar Exercise

In the following passage, there are six grammatical errors. Underline and correct them.

The organisers could have run the project themselves. After all, it was their idea. However, most of them was probably too inexperienced, and couldn't have known everything that was involved in managing such a large project or how much it would cost.

Although the sports council had given plenty of money for similar ideas in the past, last year they only give a small amount towards their project. Following this, the organisers weren't able to get no equipment, and therefore many of the training sessions had to be cancelled. As a result the clients stop coming to the centre and instead began using the facilities at the nearby business park. Problems then seemed to come their way from all directions. The organisers could have guessed what was likely to happen, but it wasn't until the letters started arriving in the post that they could finally saw the extent of their problems. When the director of the sports council actually come to see them at their office early one morning, they knew that their project was nearing the end of its time.

Discussion-based articles (including vocabulary and spelling)

The main purpose of the following exercises is to encourage the reading of, and to develop an interest in, general topic articles through which vocabulary can be expanded and spelling improved. A range of exercises can be used, relating to the articles, depending on the reading abilities of the students in the class. Initially, students can either be asked to read to themselves or to take it in turns to read out loud with a view to having their pronunciation checked and corrected as and when necessary:

'The more you have in a class, the harder the teacher's job is'

Liz Green is concerned that her three-year-old daughter, Poppy, will miss out on a place at a local primary school next year.

In the London borough of Kingston upon Thames, at least 10 of the 34 primary schools will have temporary classrooms by September.

Without them, they would not be able to squeeze in all the children aged four and five in the area, says Green, an MP's assistant and Liberal Democrat councillor.

She says her part of the borough, Surbiton, needs at least one new primary school: "Temporary classrooms are not sustainable: we need permanent ones."

Next month the borough will publish its long-term strategy on tackling the problem. Two years ago, she says, the number of children who applied to go to the primary school outstripped the number of places. Some of her friends say their children were in classes with more than 40 pupils.

"That worries me," Green says. "The more you have in a class, the harder the teacher's job is. It would be better to have an extra form."

Green, 39, is thinking not just of Poppy, who should be going to school in September next year, but also of Martha, who is one.

"We're equidistant from two good primary schools, which are half a mile to a mile away. I wouldn't want them to go to a school further away that. You are looking at buses and cars then. I want to walk them to the school gates, as my mother did for me. It's about being part of the community."

It would be easier out of London, where competition for places is less fierce.

But Green is adamant that she will stay in Surbiton: "I don't think it will end up being a problem."

Green has heard that one year, one of her preferred primary schools chose half of its pupils not because of the distance they lived from the school, but because they had siblings there. "There's nothing you can do about that, I suppose."

Jessica Shepard

Leading on from the reading then, students can be asked to:

- Underline any words they are not sure of, and check their meaning in the dictionary (likely examples will include; adamant, strategy, equidistant, siblings, sustainable etc)
- In pairs (or individually), locate and practise the spellings of the following words and phrases; temporary, permanent, assistant, September, friend, earlier, competition, worries, community, daughter, councillor, further, primary, applied, 'the borough will publish its long-term strategy', 'that worries me'

Following feedback, a whole class discussion can take place based on the article, which can in turn lead on to related issues concerning primary schools such as curriculum content and school starting age etc.

English as an Additional Language (EAL)

English for Speakers of other Languages (ESOL)

When reflecting upon the literacy and language skills of people within the country, the needs of the country's large, and increasing, immigrant community has also, naturally, to be considered. The question here that needs to be asked is, 'How does the learning experience differ for the learner who is an EAL learner from that of an English native learner developing his/her literacy skills?'

A native learner acquires the English language from a very early age, whereas an EAL learner needs to learn the language. Hawkins (1984), in contrasting mother tongue learning during infancy and foreign language learning during school, argues that the motivation for mother tongue learning is greater than for foreign language learning because there is more in the way of discovery, excitement and associated rewards. Amongst EAL learners, Wallace (1988: 4&5) outlines the difference between those 'who are learning English as a foreign rather than a second language, and have come to Britain usually specifically to improve their English' and those from 'linguistic minorities who have settled in Britain' and who 'are likely to have to function in daily life, work and education primarily through the medium of English'.

The ability of an EAL adult learner to develop their literacy skills will depend on a variety of factors including their native language literacy skills (which in turn is a reflection of their educational background), personal circumstances and degree of motivation i.e. to what degree the learners need English in their daily lives e.g. work-related reasons, integration into the community, functional reasons (going to the doctor etc.) and the amount of exposure they get to the English language in their daily lives. Wallace (1988: 3) explains that for teachers of adult literacy, functional literacy should be the goal for their learners i.e. to be aware that it's 'part of everyday life in a personal and social sense'. However, she also argues that the degree to which EAL learners, who have a different first language and culture to that of the indigenous population, need and view literacy in their everyday lives depends on their social role within their community, and backs this up by giving examples of the varying literacy expectations on an Indian housewife and a Pakistani Muslim boy.

Amongst EAL learners, naturally the range of initial levels of acquisition can be quite vast i.e. from someone who has little or no knowledge of the English language and little experience of its usage, to someone who is nearly fluent.

Furthermore, there will be a wide ability range in terms of the learners' potential to develop their English literacy skills within such a range of learners. Common learning difficulties which EAL learners experience at whatever their starting point relate to the degree to which the phonological system and grammatical structure of their own language differ from the English language. Common errors in spoken English amongst EAL learners relate to learners translating directly from their own language into English (mother tongue interference), using their native language's grammatical structures. However, the EAL learner may have strong literacy skills in their other language(s) and these are transferable but less so if the other languages use a different phonological system, and are written in scripts other than the Latin. If the first language is written in a non alphabetic script, even less so.

In comparing and contrasting the issues faced by native and non-native speakers in learning to read, Wallace (1988:64) argues that since native speakers use the English language in their daily lives and have an 'intuitive knowledge about their own language', then 'reading is not an alien code', whereas for non-native speakers, they have to use 'what they know of English to predict the structure and vocabulary of written English' and as such may have, depending on their English competence, 'difficulty in anticipating certain structures in written texts'. Furthermore, Carrell (1987) points out that amongst adults, research has shown that:

> When a reader and writer share cultural assumptions and knowledge about social systems and rituals, there is a much higher level of interaction of the reader with the text than occurs when such assumptions and knowledge are not shared.
>
> **(Carrell 1987: 43)**

Bearing in mind that those native speakers will include standard and non-standard speakers of English, it should be considered that non-standard speakers too may have language related difficulties in developing their reading and writing skills on the basis that:

> While the English writing system does not directly represent speech … the grammar of most varieties of written English is more closely related to standard English than to non-standard varieties of spoken English.
>
> **(Wallace 1988: 67)**

However, Wallace (1988: 67) also argues that 'This kind of dialectal mismatch does not appear to be, in itself, a major problem …' whilst others including Entwhisle (1978) and Bernstein (1964) have argued that those who speak non-standard English fail to benefit to the same degree as standard English speakers from formal education where standard English is the norm.

An EAL learner's native language literacy skills will also affect their English reading skills in that if they have, for example, a poor comprehension of punctuation, or a sound knowledge of punctuation conventions in the first language which are not the same as those of English, then this will serve as an additional barrier in reading to the understanding of text to that served by understanding of vocabulary and pronunciation of words; and similarly for writing, poor handwriting skills and/or a poor comprehension of punctuation, grammar and spelling rules in the EAL learner's own language will compound a learner's difficulties in writing in another language.

Native learners who wish to develop their literacy skills however, are less likely to be concerned with English language usage, but more concerned with developing their reading and writing skills. The literacy skills which need to be developed, will naturally relate (as with EAL learners) to the level of literacy skills which the native learner already has. Those skills will, in turn, relate to the learners' own educational experiences and socio-economic background, abilities and interest. The incentives for the native learner to improve their literacy skills will naturally relate to their own motivation and personal and work-related circumstances.

EAL learners are less likely to be aware of the range of non-standard English dialects that exist in the United Kingdom than a native learner, and as such, would need to be exposed during learning sessions to a range of dialects. Native learners on the other hand, who use non-standard dialects may not be aware of grammatical errors that they make in their spoken English (e.g. use of you was, 'you was', 'I done' and 'we haven't got no' etc. are all quite common in non-standard dialects), and how this may impact on their written English. Also, it should be considered that there will be many EAL learners who, due to the areas they live in, may be equally, or more likely, to accept the non-standard colloquialisms around them as standard (e.g. 'innit?').

In the early stages of literacy where a sound-letter correspondence is being taught, care should be taken to ensure that the learner has an opportunity to hear the sound. Materials intended for native speakers often assume a knowledge of vocabulary (e.g. a picture of an igloo next to the letter I), but this knowledge cannot be assumed for EAL learners. When teaching vocabulary, the meaning, spoken form of the word, and written form of the word should all be emphasised with an EAL learner. If lessons are tailored to the needs of native learners, there is a possibility of neglecting one or other of the first two. Generally speaking, EAL learners will have a smaller vocabulary, and less of an instinctive knowledge of collocation (words that go with other words) e.g. traffic jam, traffic lights, draconian measures. A strategy employed by successful readers, that of guessing from context, cannot be employed by them unless the teacher ensures that there are not too many gaps in the text i.e. limits the vocabulary load. Writing frames, prepared for a range of levels, can be a useful strategy for developing writing skills in both EAL and native learners. Examples of writing frames (writing letters, applying for courses etc.) can be found in Writing Works (2001). Both EAL and native learners could benefit from the support of pictures.

EAL learners will want to advance their knowledge of the English language alongside their literacy skills (acquiring new vocabulary and structures). In supporting general English acquisition through the written and spoken word, teachers should avoid the danger of overloading the text with unknowns and thus sabotaging the developing literacy skills. It should also be borne in mind that EAL learners who have advanced literacy skills in their own language may feel insulted by the simplicity of the content of beginner's texts. Similar sensitivity is required with adult native speakers too, as they tend not to want to read childish texts. Furthermore, EAL learners who do read well in their other language(s) should be explicitly taught how to use a bilingual dictionary.

When reflecting on theories of language and development in order to choose an approach that would best enable any given learner to develop their literacy skills, it can be considered that according to Knowles (1998: 22), 'Learning theories fall into two major families: *behaviourist/connectionist theories* and *cognitive/gestalt theories*' Whereas cognitive development theories relate to understanding why adult learners have difficulties in dealing with quite advanced issues (Knowles 1998), behaviourist theories are based on the idea that learning is a function of change in overt behaviour and that those changes are the result of an individual's response to events (stimuli) that occur in the environment. The theory, as applied to language development, centres around the idea that a stimulus (such as the first sentence of a dialogue) meets with a response and that if that stimulus and response is praised or rewarded by the teacher, a stimulus-response pattern can be established with a learner which conditions that particular learner to respond in future instances. Reinforcement is the key element in the stimulus-response theory, where the reinforcement is anything that strengthens the desired response e.g. verbal praise, a good grade etc.

For a learner who is illiterate, language practice should take the form of question (stimulus) and answer (response) frames which expose students to the language in gradual steps. This requires that the learner makes a response for every frame and receives immediate feedback in the form of positive reinforcement on the basis that behaviour that is positively reinforced will reoccur. If a learner is illiterate, it is likely that they will have arrived in the UK as an immigrant or refugee from a rural community within a developing country (in Africa or Asia) where literacy is not as highly valued as it would be in other types of community. As such, there is a likelihood that the learner will have come from a tradition where although oral fluency would be important, literacy skills such as reading and writing are less valued, particularly for women. Furthermore, if a learner is illiterate in their own language, it is likely that their language skills will have been acquired in an informal way rather than learnt in a formal manner. Krashen (1981) outlines the difference between 'language acquisition' (the natural assimilation of language rules through using language for communication) and 'language learning' (the formal study of language rules as a conscious process).

In terms of theories of language learning, an approach which could be considered for an illiterate learner is the 'interactional view', whereby according to Richards and Rodgers (2001: 21), language is seen 'as a vehicle for the realization of interpersonal relations and for the performance of social transactions between individuals' and therefore 'as a tool for the creation and maintenance of social relations'.

An illiterate person will initially need the native language to 'survive' in a community i.e. to be able to interact with others in carrying out everyday functions such as shopping, accessing services and finding a job etc. It is important therefore that learning reflects realistic everyday life situations. In discussing adult learning theory, Knowles (1998) states that:

> 'Adults are motivated to learn as they experience needs and interests that learning will satisfy' and that 'Adults orientation to learning is life-centred; therefore, the appropriate units for organising adult learning are life situations, not subjects.
>
> **(Knowles 1998: 40)**

In distinguishing between theories of learning and theories of teaching, Gagne (1985) has argued that while learning theories address methods of learning, teaching theories address the methods employed to influence learning.

An example of such a method, which is based on the learning theory of behaviourism (discussed above) is the 'audio-lingual method'. According to Harmer (1991: 32), the method makes 'constant drilling of the students followed by positive or negative reinforcement a major focus of classroom activity'. Basing the methodology on the stimulus-response-reinforcement model, mistakes are, according to Harmer (1991: 32) 'immediately criticised, and correct utterances … immediately praised.'

Other teaching methodologies focus more on the humanistic aspects of learning, whereby it is argued that language teaching should, in focusing on learners' experiences, look to develop themselves as people and encourage positive feelings (Harmer 1991). Advocates of humanistic approaches then would, according to Harmer (1991: 36) tend to use classroom activities that made learners 'feel good and … remember happy times and events whilst at the same time practising language'. In terms of classroom activities that could be used to develop an illiterate learner's aural skills, it should be borne in mind that, according to Ur (1984: 35), 'a grasp of the phonology of the new language is a fairly basic requisite for learning to speak it' and also a prerequisite for later developing sound-written symbol relationships. With this in mind, she advocates listening exercises whereby the learner is given the opportunity to practise 'identifying correctly different sounds, sound-combinations and intonations'.

In order that the focus will be predominantly on developing the learner's aural perception skills, Ur (1984: 35) suggests minimising visual stimuli and 'contextual clues to meaning' through use of a range of recordings rather than live speech. At the word level then, the learner practises listening to and repeating words in isolation from each other. Time should be built into the activities by the teacher for error correction and positive feedback to the learner.

At sentence level however, the difficulties for a learner increases as aural perception is hampered by the idiosyncrasies of English speech, such as word contractions, unstressed syllables, elision of consonants and variation in vowel sounds. In order to further develop the learner's aural skills, activities need now to be focused on sensitising the learner to the 'blurring' of words that takes place in spoken discourse due to the above. The learner needs to listen to and repeat short phrases or sentences, still ensuring, as above, that they rely predominantly on their ear. Further aural activities can include; listening to recordings of short sentences and answering the question, 'how many words?', and listening to recordings of short sentences and asking if certain facts are true or false. Care should be taken to ensure that there is not too much in the way of new language or utterances introduced into each session that may 'overload' the learner, and that time is allowed for continual error correction and feedback to the learner.

On the basis that both the above activities rely on a stimulus (the learner hearing words or sentences) and a response (repetition of the word or sentence), error correction, drilling and positive reinforcement, I would argue that they lend themselves towards the audio-lingual teaching method and are hence based on a behaviourist learning model.

I have spent the past few years teaching ESOL part-time in evening classes to adult students in an inner-city college. The students come from a variety of backgrounds, the majority coming from countries across the Asian sub-continent and eastern Europe. Naturally, any group of learners starting a class will come from a variety of backgrounds and be motivated to learn English through a mixture of intrinsic and extrinsic factors. As such, the learners within a class will vary in their ability to learn. As far as it is possible, learners are banded together in a class following an initial assessment of their speaking and listening, reading and writing skills, against criteria relating to a given level. Most are at entry 2 or entry 3 level, are literate in their own language and have been living in the country from a few months to a few years (although some have been living here for many years). The individual learners (and the classes as a whole) have always been exceptionally courteous, making them a pleasure to teach. I often encourage and nag my classes to engage more in the English language i.e. to read as wide a range of texts as possible and to practise speaking the language with people outside of the college. One thing I reflect on however is the lack of pressure exerted on them by society in general and employers in particular to improve their language skills. This I believe is a factor in preventing many ESOL learners from integrating fully into British communities.

I often begin classes by focusing on common, everyday questions and answers, and expressions, that the learner is likely to be familiar with, and which do not require any broad knowledge of grammar or tenses, such as, 'How are you?', 'What is your name?', 'What time is it?' and 'Where are your from?' etc By restricting the variation in the grammar within the questions and answers to the components of the verb 'to be', a tutor is able to focus on developing their learners' fluency.

For example, students should get used to the sound of contractions early on, and be given the opportunity to practise listening and responding to questions with them. As well as being encouraged to use contractions in speech, they should learn how to recognise and write with (and without) them.

Attention should also be paid at this stage to the pronunciation of unstressed syllables in speech, as a means of improving learners' fluency. Due to the nature of English as a 'stress-timed' language, it is common for an ESOL learner to miss out or 'pass over' unstressed syllables such as 'a', 'the', ''m', 'are' and 'to'. The location and importance of these syllables can be reinforced through reading and writing exercises which clearly highlight the position of the unstressed syllables.

Present tense (everyday questions)

How **are** you? I **am** fine thanks I**'m** fine thanks
What **is** your name? What**'s** your name? My name **is**... My name's...
What **is** his name? What**'s** his name? His name **is**... His name**'s**...
Where **are** you from? I **am** from... I**'m** from...
Where **is** he from? Where**'s** he from? He **is** from... He**'s** from...
Where **is** she from? Where**'s** she from? She **is** from... She**'s** from ...
Where **are** they from? They **are** from ...
What time **is** it? It **is** ten past eight. It**'s** ten past eight.
What **is** the date today? It **is** the 12th of July
What**'s** the date today? It**'s** the 22nd of August
What **is** your job? I **am** a...
What**'s** your job? I**'m** a...
How old **are** you? I **am** 26 years old. I**'m** 26 years old.
Where**'s** the pen? It**'s** on the desk.
Where **are** the pens? They **are** on the desk.
Where**'s** the book? It**'s** on the shelf
Where**'s** the nearest toilet please? It**'s** down the corridor on the right.
Is there a supermarket nearby? Yes, there**'s** on in the centre of town.
Are there many people in town today? Yes there **are** (many people in town today). No there **aren't** (many people in town today).
Are there any mountains in your country? Yes there **are** (mountains in my country).
No there **aren't** (any mountains in my country). Etc

The verb used to form the above sentences is, **'To Be'** which is:

I am	We are (Kate and I are)
You are (s)	You are (pl)
He is (Fred is)	They are (James and Sarah are)
She is (Jane is)	
It is (The car is; My idea is; etc)	

In the above, there isn't much change in the grammatical structure, but there is room to increase vocabulary (e.g. objects around the room, or professions) in degrees appropriate to the abilities of the students within the class.

On the basis that many learners will not necessarily have the level of English to understand explanations regarding tenses, they will need to be demonstrated, and learnt through use i.e. combining speaking and listening, reading and writing exercises. Use of tenses can be learnt in the context of comparing the use of one tense in relation to another. For example, the present continuous can be explained through illustrating what is happening at the present moment ('now') or through describing momentary, or temporary, actions. This can be compared and contrasted with the simple present, which can be explained through illustrating events that happen all the time or sometimes, or that are true in general. The use of the present continuous in describing momentary actions, can be illustrated through pictures, such as in the following examples, then compared and contrasted with the use of the simple present:

Look at the pictures on the previous page.

Picture **1** (present continuous):
What's he do**ing**? He's teach**ing**.

Picture **2** (present continuous):
What's she do**ing**? She's work**ing** on the computer.

Picture **3** (present continuous):
What are they do**ing**? They're hav**ing** a meeting.

Picture 4 (present continuous):
Is it rain**ing** outside? Yes it is (rain**ing** outside).

The present simple:

1. He teaches part-time in the college.
2. She works on the computer every day.
3. They have a meeting every Thursday afternoon.
4. It usually rains in Autumn.

A way of further helping students to distinguish between the use of these 'paired' tenses, can be to highlight how the use of the subject and verb in the answer reflects the question. A common mistake made by ESOL learners in their spoken English is to omit the verb 'to be' from the present continuous, for example, *'I going to town later.'* Naturally, in the context of delivering learning in an ESOL class, such errors should be constantly and consistently corrected, and the proper use of the present continuous reinforced through structured written exercises. The exercise on page .. (Correcting mistakes made in everyday spoken English) for example, gives learners the opportunity to identify and correct such errors (in spoken and written English).

Present continuous Vs Present simple

Present Continuous

What are you do**ing** now?
I'm learn**ing** English; I'm sitt**ing** down; I'm read**ing** a newspaper; I'm looking at the board; I'm listening to music; I'm working on the computer.

What's Abdul do**ing**?
He's learn**ing** English; He's play**ing** football; He's play**ing** on the computer.

What's he do**ing**?
He's learn**ing** English; He's watch**ing** TV; He is fill**ing** in an application form.

What are they do**ing**?
They are play**ing** cricket; They're go**ing** shopping; They're walk**ing** home.

Is the computer work**ing**?
Yes, it is (work**ing**). No, it isn't (work**ing**).

Are the trains running on time?
Yes, they are (running on time). No, they're not (runn**ing** on time). Etc

Present simple

Where do you work? I work in Milton Keynes.

Where does he work? He works in Milton Keynes

Where does John work? He works in Milton Keynes.

What time do you get up in the morning? I usually get up at half past seven.

What time does she get up in the morning? She gets up at half past seven.

What time does Helen get up in the morning? She gets up at half past seven.

Do you like coffee? Yes, **I do** (like coffee). No, **I don't** (like coffee).

Does he take milk and sugar? Yes, **he does**. No, he doesn't.

Do they go there often? Yes, **they do**. No, **they don't**. Etc.

The verb that needs to be learnt in the context of the above tense is 'to do', as an auxiliary (or supplementary) verb, including in its negative form, interrogative and negative interrogative forms, since its structure, in each of these forms, can frequently cause difficulties with ESOL learners. A common error with the third person singular interrogative for example is to use the 's' ending twice e.g. Does he likes his present? The exercise on P84 (correcting mistakes made in everyday spoken English) includes examples whereby such errors can be identified and corrected (in spoken and written English).

To do

I do	We do (Paul and I do)
You do (s)	You do (pl)
He does (Michael does)	They do (Johanna and Graham do)
She does (Sarah does)	
It does (The car does)	

I don't	We don't (Paul and I don't)
You don't (s)	You don't (pl)
He doesn't (Michael doesn't)	They don't (Johanna and Graham don't)
She doesn't (Sarah doesn't)	
It doesn't (The car doesn't)	

Do I?	Do we? (Do Paul and I?)
Do you? (s)	Do you? (pl)
Does he? (Does Michael?)	Do they? (Do Johanna and Graham?)
Does she? (Does Sarah?)	
Does it? (Does the car?)	

Don't I?	Don't we? (Do Paul and I?)
Don't you? (s)	Don't you? (pl)
Doesn't he? (Does Michael?)	Don't they? (Do Johanna and Graham?)
Doesn't she? (Does Sarah?)	
Doesn't it? (Doesn't the car?)	

Throughout the learners' learning process, the tutor should ensure constant and consistent correction of errors, such as those indicated above related to developing their learners' fluency and pronunciation generally. If, as is commonly the case with students developing their spoken English skills, they find themselves hesitating or pausing between particular words in a sentence which do not require a pause, then a line (/) can be put through the written sentence on the board to indicate where the hesitation is occurring. When this has been done, the learner can be given the opportunity to practise blending the two relevant syllables either side of the pause. This procedure can further help develop learners' fluency.

Present continuous Vs Past continuous

Here, the use of the **present continuous** can be elaborated on and developed to include the future. This can be best explained through linking its use with a time reference, for example:

What are you do**ing** tomorrow? I'm work**ing** all day; **I'm** go**ing to** town;

I'm going shopp**ing**; **I'm** visit**ing** my friend

When are you go**ing to** Pakistan? We**'re** go**ing** there in the summer;

When **is** he start**ing** his course? He**'s** starting **it** next week;

What**'s** she do**ing** later? She**'s** go**ing to** the theatre. Etc.

This can be compared with the use of the **past continuous**, which can be explained in the context of putting across the idea that you are describing a continuous action that was happening in the past. For example:

What were you do**ing** yesterday afternoon?

I was work**ing**. I was watch**ing** TV

What were they do**ing** yesterday evening?

They were work**ing**. They were watch**ing** TV.

Where was she go**ing** earlier?

She was go**ing** into town. She was go**ing** to the library.

Who was Colin meet**ing** last night?

He was meet**ing** his girlfriend. He was meet**ing** his colleagues. Etc.

Again, the use of the verb in the answer can be shown to reflect its use in the question. The past continuous can be further illustrated through its use after 'while' and 'when'. For example:

'While I was cooking, I burnt myself.'

'I saw you when you were swimming.'

'She called while I was sleeping.'

'They arrived while I was taking a shower.'

As with the present continuous, a common error made by ESOL learners using the past continuous is to omit the verb 'to be', for example, *'I working yesterday.'* As with errors made in the use of the present continuous, errors made in the use of the past continuous should be constantly and consistently corrected, and its proper use reinforced through structured written exercises.

Past continuous Vs Simple past

In order to explain the use of the **simple past**, you can put across the idea that you are describing an action that has been completed, and compared with the above for the past continuous. For example:

What **did you do** yesterday afternoon? **I went** to the cinema.
I went shopping.

What **did Jean do** yesterday afternoon?

She went to the cinema. **She went** shopping.

Where **did you have** lunch? **I had** it in the school canteen.

What **did you have** for lunch?

I had fried chicken and chips. **I had** a lasagne with a salad.

What **did she have** for lunch?

She had fried chicken and chips. **She had** a lasagne with a salad.

Who **did you see** at school this morning?

I saw the headmaster. **I saw** my son's form teacher.

Who **did he see** at school this morning?

He saw the headmaster. **He saw** his son's form teacher.

Did you go out last night?

Yes **I did** (go out last night). No **I didn't** (go out last night).

Did she collect her car? Yes **she did**. No **she didn't**.

Did he meet his friend? Yes **he did**. No **he didn't**.

Did they win the match? Yes **they did**. No **they didn't**. Etc

Common errors in the use of the simple past, include using the past form twice, for example:

'Did you saw him?'

'I didn't went to the cinema.'

Past simple Vs Present perfect

The use of the **present perfect** (have + past participle) can be explained in the context of describing an event which has finished in the recent past (or is unfinished), whereas with the simple past, there is a specific time reference, for example: last week, yesterday, in April 1994, a month ago etc. With the present perfect, we often use the following time adverbials: yet, already, recently, just, never, lately, ever etc.

Have you ever **been** to America? Yes *or* Yes, I have
(*means* yes, **I have been** to America).

Have you heard of John Lennon? No *or* No, I haven't
(*means* no, **I haven't heard of** John Lennon).

I have never eaten marmite. *c.f.* late marmite last week.
She has just arrived. *c.f.* She arrived at 3 o'clock.

We have never been to Paris.
I have lived in England for 3 years.
We have known each other for 2 weeks.
He has worked there since September.
I have already told you.
She has already eaten.
We have not finished yet.

The verb that needs to be learnt in the context of the above tense is 'to have', as an auxiliary (or supplementary) verb, including in its negative form, interrogative and negative interrogative forms as its structure, in each of these forms, can frequently cause difficulties with ESOL learners:

To have

I have	We have (Paul and I have)
You have (s)	You have (pl)
He has (Michael has)	They have (Johanna and Graham have)
She has (Sarah has)	
It has (The computer has)	

I haven't	We haven't (Paul and I haven't)
You haven't (s)	You haven't (pl)
He hasn't (Michael hasn't)	They haven't (Johanna and Graham haven't)
She hasn't (Sarah hasn't)	
It hasn't (The computer hasn't)	

Have I?	Have we? (Have Paul and I?)
Have you? (s)	Have you? (pl)
Has he? (Has Michael?)	Have they (Have Johanna and Graham?)
Has she? (Has Sarah?)	
Has it? (Has the computer?)	

Haven't I?	Haven't we? (Have Paul and I?)
Haven't you? (s)	Haven't you? (pl)
Hasn't he? (Has Michael?)	Haven't they (Haven't Johanna and Graham?)
Hasn't she? (Hasn't Sarah?)	
Hasn't it? (Hasn't the computer?)	

As stated earlier, the importance of constant and continuous error correction can not be over emphasised. Further 'paired' tenses can be compared and taught together, such as 'Present perfect Vs Past perfect' etc. In order to consolidate learning of the tenses, exercises such as those on P81 and P82 can be used.

Learners also need to be given the opportunity to learn, through practice (speaking and listening, and reading and writing), the simple past and past participles of the most common regular and irregular verbs, which can be found listed in many language textbooks.

Naturally, if you're in a position, and you have the time, to record learners' spoken English with a view to providing detailed and constructive feedback to assist their language development, then this should be done. Below is the transcript of a conversation with a learner in my class, followed by an analysis of the transcribed data and recommendations for developing the learner's language skills. This is followed by an analysis of the learner's reading, and an analysis of a piece of writing submitted by the learner. The learner in question is a 28 year old Polish man, who has been living in Britain for 1 year. He left school at 18, having obtained a place at a nearby university where he studied business studies for 4 years. He gives the impression that he had a relatively comfortable lifestyle in Poland. Nevertheless, he wanted to come to Britain in order to work for more money, and realised that improving his English would help him achieve a better job.

The learner joined the Entry level 2 ESOL conversational English class in January '07 having been initially assessed (in reading and writing) at Entry level 2. The learner comes across as quite confident and will, whether responding to a question from the tutor or from another student in a prepared text, often go 'off script' i.e. add additional words or phrases in order to 'show off' his knowledge. Similarly, he is often one of the first students to contribute an opinion to open class discussions, particularly if the discussion is based around a subject he is interested in (such as sport or Polish customs).

Transcription of Taped Recording between tutor (T) and ESOL learner (L)

1 <T> Um I know you're from Poland. Which part of Poland are you from again?
2 <L> I am from uh south west Poland.
3 <T> OK. Um what's the name of your town?
4 <L> Um my town names it's uh Swidniza.
5 <T> Schwid?
6 <L> Swidniza.
7 <T> OK. Can you describe your town? Is it a big place small place?
8 <L> No it's a small town about sixty thousand people
9 <T> OK. That's great. Um six thousand people so …
10 <L> Sixty
11 <T> Sixty thousand people
12 <L> Sixty thousand people
13 <T> So it's a small town?
14 <L> Yes small town
15 <T> And can you describe it? What's what … what is it like there?
16 <L> (silence – 2 secs)
17 <T> What is it like there?
18 <L> (silence – 6 secs)
19 <T> Can you describe the town? Tell me about the town?
20 <L> (silence – 4 secs)
21 <T> Are the people there friendly?
22 <L> Yes people is very friendly this is a … a small town

23 <T> Yeah
24 <L> And … everybody know everything about the other person
25 <T> OK, yeah I know the type of place.
26 <L> This is a beautiful town with a um new city centre rest restaurant
27 <T> Yeah OK that's great and um are you in the country? Is it in the countryside?
28 <L> (silence – 5 secs)
29 <T> Is it near other towns or is there much country like grass trees outside?
30 <L> Yes … (inaudible)
31 <T> OK um and have you been back to Poland recently?
32 <L> Er the last time I been to Poland er 6, 7 months ago
33 <T> OK, that's fine good um and so how long have you been in England for?
34 <L> Now I am here er one year
35 <T> One year OK good and in Poland … do you have um a good education system there?
36 <L> Yes er we have a good education system
37 <T> OK that's great and you're … I think you told me before that you're working, so what is your job here?
38 <L> Er now I working on the mortgage paper company I am lorry driver
39 <T> Yeah, and do you like your job?
40 <L> Yes I like
41 <T> OK and what sort of hours are you doing?
42 <L> Er usually I working er 9 hours a day
43 <T> From?
44 <L> From half past er five to half past (inaudible (seven?))
45 <T> OK that's fine and um sorry and er how long have you been working where you are?
46 <L> Here?
47 <T> Yes
48 <L> Er I working here 11 er months
49 <T> OK good and er you … you live in Luton?
50 <L> Yes I live in Luton
51 <T> OK and do you have any brothers or sisters?
52 <L> Yes I have one sister
53 <T> OK.
54 <L> She's name Evelina
55 <T> OK and um is she married?

56 <L> Yes I am married

57 <T> No is she married?

58 <L> Er Evelina?

59 <T> Yes

60 <L> No she's not married

61 <T> OK and I was just about to ask you are you married?

62 <L> Yes I am married

63 <T> OK and er how long have you been married for?

64 <L> Er I am married 6 years

65 <T> OK great and um sorry going back to your sister I know it's the other way round now you said um does she speak good English?

66 <L> My sister?

67 <T> Yes

68 <L> Yes she very good speak English

70 <T> OK better than you?

71 <L> Yes more than me

72 <T> OK um when you came to you came to England about a year ago what did your friends think about you coming to England?

73 <L> (silence – 4 secs) I don't know it's (inaudible)

74 <T> About you coming to England about about you coming to England

75 <L> Very big surprise for somebody (inaudible)

76 <T> OK

77 <L> Somebody uh going better better life Poland (inaudible)

78 <T> Yeah that's fine OK good and um OK and what what did you use to do in Poland?

79 <L> The last my job in Poland uh managing director

80 <T> Managing director?

81 <L> Yes

82 <T> Yeah

83 <L> Um I recruit people training people and planning media relation

84 <T> Managing?

85 <L> Uh media relation

86 <T> OK media relation

87 <L> Yes media relation

88 <T> OK and was that a worthwhile job?

89 <L> Sorry

90 <T> Was that a worthwhile job?

91 <L> (silence – 3 secs)

92 <T> Um was that did you was that a good job?

93 <L> Yes very good job

94 <T> OK and um now you're working in England what kind of work would you like to do if you had the choice (pause) here?

95 <L> Well if I have if I have the choice

96 <T> Yeah

97 <L> I would like to do the same work in Poland

98 <T> OK

99 <L> But you know I must learn English

100 <T> Yeah OK good and um what do you do in your spare time here? What do you do in your spare time?

101 <L> Spare time?

102 <T> Your free time here?

103 <L> I spend my time with my family at home and my wife we going to the park uh we giving food for bird

104 <T> For?

105 <L> Bird bird

106 <T> OK yeah yeah good yeah yeah yeah

107 <L> (inaudible)

108 <T> OK do you travel around have you travelled around England much?

109 <L> Yes uh everyday I travel around England

110 <T> Yeah

111 <L> Cos everyday I I making about three four hundred miles

112 <T> OK (pause) everyday?

113 <L> Yeah

114 <T> Yeah OK so where where do you travel to in England? All all everywhere?

115 <L> Usually I going to Essex

116 <T> Yeah

117 <L> Lincolnshire

118 <T> Yeah

119 <L> North Northampton Buckinghamshire Hertfordshire and London

120 <T> So you know the M1 very well

121 <L> Yeah (laughing)

122 <T> And and the A1 maybe

123 <L> (inaudible) M1 very well

124 <T> Yeah OK

125 <L> Specially after all (inaudible)

126 <T> OK and do you like cooking?

127 <L> Yes I I like cooking

128 <T> And what's your favourite?

129 <L> I cooking very well

130 <T> Yeah OK and what's your favourite dish?

131 <L> Umm my favourite it's er spaghetti

132 <T> Yeah yeah yeah

133 <L> Spaghetti bolognaise

134 <T> OK yeah good and do you prefer Polish or English food?

135 <L> Polish (pause) Polish

136 <T> And um do you like listening to music?

137 <L> Yes I like listening to music

138 <T> And what sort of music do you like?

139 <L> I lik e rhythm and blues especially

140 <T> Yeah

141 <L> I like very like er the Rolling Stones

142 <T> Yeah

143 <L> And Pink Floyd er Dire Straits and …

144 <T> So you're you're an old rocker then?

145 <L> Yeah

146 <T> (laughing) OK excellent and um do you like wearing fashionable clothes?

147 <L> (pause) yes yes

148 <T> OK good um OK and you've been coming to this English class for a while now where where do you normally um sit in the class?

149 <L> (pause) I normally sit on the back

150 <T> OK and how do you find the the other people in the class?

151 <L> (silence – 3 secs)

152 <T> What do you think about the other people in the class?

153 <L> What I think?

154 <T> Yeah

155 <L> It's very people is very friendly I like these people

156 <T> OK that's great OK I think that that's good that's excellent … and just one more question Dariusz um when you speak English everyday at work or (inaudible) do English people ever correct you?

157 <L> No nobody don't correct me

158 <T> No never?

159 <L> Never

160 <T> Apart from me
161 <L> Yes
162 <T> (laughing) OK thanks

Analysis of Transcribed Data

Grammar

The learner's native language is Polish, and on the basis that it is a Slavonic language related to Russian (Monk and Burak 1987) and sharing many of its grammatical and phonological features, it will be assumed that references to grammatical or phonological features relating to Russian learners in any text (e.g. the chapter on 'Russian speakers' in Monk and Borak 1987) will also apply to Polish learners.

The learner makes errors in his speech with the use of the present simple tense. For example, on 103, the learner says '... we going to the park' instead of '... we go to the park', on 111 '... I making three four hundred miles' instead of '... I make three four hundred miles' and on 129 'I cooking very well' instead of 'I cook very well'. In the Adult ESOL Core Curriculum (2001), it states (section Lr/E2) that *'Adults should learn to:* respond to requests for information' and in so doing:

> 'recognise questions of the *wh-* type and ... recognise verb forms and time markers to understand the time to which a speaker is referring and respond appropriately, e.g. (a) present simple ...
>
> **(DfES 2001: 132)**

The learner makes errors in his speech with the use of the present perfect tense. For example, in response to the question (33) ' ... how long have you been in England for?' the learner replies (34), ' ... I am here ... one year' instead of, 'I have been here for one year' and in response to the question (63) '... how long have you been married for?' the learner replies (64) '... I am married for 6 years' instead of 'I have been married for 6 years'. The DfES (2001) states (section Sc/E3) that:

> '*Adults should learn to:* ask questions to obtain personal or factual information ... in a range of tenses, e.g.: (a) present perfect
>
> **(DfES 2001: 182)**

The learner also makes errors in his speech with the use of the present perfect continuous tense. For example, in response to the question (45) '... how long have you been working where you are?' the learner replies (48) ' … I working here er 11 months' instead of 'I have been working here for 11 months'.

The reasons for the above errors relate to the fact that Slavonic languages have, according to Monk and Borak (1987: 122) 'no present perfect or present progressive forms' and that they have 'only one simple present tense'.

The learner makes errors in his speech with the subject verb agreement. For example, on 22 and 155, the learner says '… people is very friendly…' instead of 'people are very friendly, on 24 '… everybody know everything…' instead of 'everybody knows everything…', and on 68 '… she very good speak English' instead of 'she speaks English very well'. The DfES (2001) states (section Ws/E3) that:

> *Adults should learn to:* use basic sentence grammar accurately – understand that a verb and its subject must agree …
>
> **(DfES 2001: 240)**

The learner makes errors during the dialogue with the word order of adjectives. For example, on 79 the learner says 'the last my job in Poland' instead of 'my last job in Poland' and on 68, '… she very good speak English' instead of '… she speaks very good English'. The DfES (2001) states (section Ws/E2) that:

> *Adults should learn to:* use appropriate word order in simple and compound sentences, and be aware of how this may differ from word order in their other languages
>
> **(DfES 2001: 158)**

In Polish/Russian, the word order is noun + adjective. The learner makes errors during the dialogue with prepositions. For example, on 38, the learner says, '… I working on the Moorgate Paper Company…' instead of 'I am working for the Moorgate Paper Company' and on 149, 'I normally sit on the back' instead of 'I normally sit at the back'. The learner also makes errors in his speech through the omission of articles. For example, on 24 the learner says 'yes people is very friendly' instead of 'yes the people are very friendly' and on 38, '… I am lorry driver' instead of '… I am a lorry driver'. The DfES (2001) states (section Sc/E2) that:

> *Adults should learn to:* express statements of fact – use with some accuracy grammatical forms suitable for the levels, e.g. (c) prepositions of place and time (d) indefinite and definite article.
>
> **(DfES 2001: 110)**

Monk and Burak (1987: 126) argue that for Slavonic learners, 'The use of prepositions often results in errors'. One of the reasons for the learners difficulties with articles is the fact that there are no articles in the Polish language. As Monk and Burak (1987: 125) state, 'One of the initial problems for … learners is learning how to use articles in general'. However, the learner uses articles correctly in much of the conversation e.g on 8, '… it's a small town …', on 149, ' I normally sit on the back' and on 137, 'I like listening to music'.

The learner makes an error on 71, with the use of the comparative adjective. In responding to the question '… better than you?', referring to whether or not his English was better than his sister's, the learner replies 'yes more than me' instead of 'yes better than me'. Monk and Burak (1987:125) state that Slavonic speakers have 'difficulties … in the formation of the degrees of comparison of the adjectives *bad, good* and *far'*. The DfES (2001: 116) states that *'Adults should learn to:* - be able to make comparisons, using comparative adjectives, both with *–er* and with *more'*

The learner makes errors during the dialogue with the use of deictic markers e.g. whilst talking about his home town in Poland on 22, the learner says '… this is a … a small town' instead of 'it's a small town' and on 155, in response to how he finds the other people in the class, the says ' I like these people' instead of 'I like them'. The DfES (2001: 132) states that *'Adults should learn to:* understand some deictic markers, e.g. this, that, here, there'.

Other grammatical errors include the misuse of the pronoun and misuse of the common rule of the genitive (to express possession i.e. 's) on 54 where the learner says 'she's name Evelina' instead of 'her name is Evelina'.

In order to develop the learner's understanding and correct use of the above verb tenses and grammatical forms, the learner could first be allowed to listen to the recorded conversation and be given the opportunity to correct his mistakes. If the mistakes are not identified (or only partly identified), the learner should then be given the opportunity to read the transcript of the taped recording between tutor and learner, and again be given the chance to identify his own mistakes.

In supporting the learner's literacy development, a range of activities/tasks should be demonstrated by the tutor. In each case, the target language should be presented clearly with the use of appropriate models and the learner given the opportunity to practice through repetition. Krashen (1981: 2) argues that, 'Conscious language learning … is thought to be helped a great deal by error correction and the presentation of explicit rules' and that, 'Error correction … helps the learner come to the correct mental representation of the linguistic generalization'.

In addition, a series of structured written exercises should be given, such as those from Murphy (1997: 18) in order to reinforce the correct use of the relevant tense or grammatical form. These exercises can be supplemented by the DfES's (2003) ESOL Skills for Life materials, which place the learning of the relevant tense or grammatical form into an everyday context through a series of speaking and listening, and writing exercises. In so doing, a variety of learning styles can be taken into consideration.

Discourse Features

Reflecting on the learner's use of language in the transcript, it can be seen that a variety of common discourse features are used including:

Fillers (um, uh etc.) e.g. on 4, '**um** my town … it's **uh** …' and 32, '**er** the last time I been to Poland **er** 6, 7 months ago'

Discourse markers, which according to Carter and McCarthy (1997: 14), 'help speakers to negotiate their way through talk …' e.g. on 95, the learner says '**well** if I have … the choice' and 99, 'but **you know** I must learn English'. Carter and McCarthy (1997: 14) also state that 'In conversation in general phrases such as *you know* … serve to check understanding and to soften and personalise the interactive style …'. Furthermore, the DfES (2001: 112) states that '*Adults should learn to:* give personal information – know and use discourse markers to introduce a response, especially in informal situations, e.g. *well*.'

Deixis, which according to Carter and McCarthy (1997: 13), '… describes what may be termed the orientational features of language' e.g. on 38, the learner says 'er **now** I working …'. Carter and McCarthy (1997: 13) also state that '… words like *now* and *then* relate to the current moment of utterance… '. However, as explained above, the learner also makes errors with the use of deictic markers.

Adverbs e.g. '**usually**' which appears on 42 and 115 and '**normally**' on 149. Carter and McCarthy (1997: 12) state that 'words like … *usually* … are used frequently by speakers to indicate personal attitudes and judgements' and that in so doing, they 'play an important part in … modifying whole propositions'.

Phonological patterns

On 26 and 52, the short vowel sound /ɪ/ in 'c**i**ty' and 's**i**ster' is pronounced more like the long vowel /iː/. On 83 and 85, the long vowel sound /iː/ in m**e**dia is pronounced more like the short vowel /e/. On 103, the long vowel sound /ɜː/ in 'b**ir**d' is pronounced more like the short vowel /ɪ/ followed by the consonant /r/. The reason for the above is because, according to Monk and Barak (1987: 117), one of the main features which distinguishes English from the Slavonic sound system is 'the absence of the short-long vowel differentiation'.

On 38, 42 and 48, the long vowel sound /ɜː/ in 'w**or**king' is pronounced slightly differently. The difficulty for the learner in the pronunciation of this phoneme, is due to the fact that it doesn't have an equivalent sound in slavonic languages (Monk and Barat 1987). The pronunciation is perhaps similar to a vowel in the learner's native language (Polish).

On 3, the learner has difficulty pronouncing the 'th' in 'sou**th**' correctly (the interdental), and likewise with the 'th' in '**th**ousand' on 8. In both cases, the pronunciation tends towards 't'. Monk and Borak (1987: 118) explain that this difficulty is due to the absence of the sound (Theta) in Slavonic languages. On 32 and 48, the learner has difficulty in pronouncing the 'ths' in mon**ths**. In both cases, it sounds like 'mon**ts**'. Monk and Borak (1987: 119) argue that the combination of 'th' and 's' (as in months or clothes) is 'generally a major challenge even for quite good learners, who often tend to substitute /ts/'.

On 50, the learner pronounces the place name 'Luton' incorrectly by pronouncing the the vowel 'o' between the 't' and the 'n'. Monk and Burak (1987: 119) point out that Slavonic speakers 'tend to insert the neutral sound /ə/ in the combinations /tl/, /dl/, /tn/...' However, in this case, the learner appears to have inserted the /ɒ/ sound.

In terms of word stress, the learner is, in general, consistent with where he places stress on each word. For example, for high frequency nouns, such as people (22), centre (26) and family (103), and adjectives such as Polish (135) and favourite (131) the learner tends to place stress on the first syllable, and for high frequency verbs such as working (38 and 42) and cooking (127 and 129), the learner tends to place stress on the second syllable. However, in long English place names with suffixes (e.g. Hertfordshire), the suffix (i.e. shire) is not normally stressed. However, on 117, and 119, the learner can clearly be heard placing stress on the suffixes (shire) of the place names Lincolnshire, Buckinghamshire and Hertfordshire.

In terms of sentence stress on 58 (er Evelina?) and 66 (my sister?), the learner uses rising intonation towards the end of each sentence/word to indicate the interrogative. On 8, in responding to the question 'Is it a big place?', (relating to the size of his home town) the learner replies in the negative and places the stress at the beginning of the sentence ('no it's a small town about sixty thousand people'), and the intonation therefore declines. Similarly, on 40 (yes I like), 68 (yes she very good speak English), and 93 (yes very good job) when replying to questions in the affirmative, the learner places the stress at the beginning of each sentence and the intonation declines. In each of the above answers that the learner gives, the intonation/sentence stress occurs as a result of the learner's enthusiasm for the subject matter. In much of the dialogue however, the intonation and sentence stress is fairly consistent.

In terms of sentence rhythm, Monk and Burak (1987: 119) argue that it can present difficulties for learners, and cite the example of how 'learners often pronounce the slower 'strong' forms of words like *as, than, can, must* or *have* instead of the faster 'weak' forms. Listening to the transcript, it is clear that the slower, stronger form of the word 'have' (36 and 52) is pronounced, and likewise with 'than' (72).

Relating to the above, the DfES (2001) states (section Sc/E2) that:

> *Adults should learn to:* articulate the sounds of English to make meaning understood – distinguish between similar-sounding phonemes, to make meaning clear
>
> **DfES (2001: 102)**

In addition, it states that:

> *Adults should learn to:* use stress and intonation adequately to make speech comprehensible and meaning understood – develop awareness that English has a stress-timed rhythm and make a distinction between stressed and unstressed syllables in their own words
>
> **DfES (2001: 102)**

To that end the DfES (2001: 103) recommends a range of sample activities in order to assist learners with the above, including; listening 'to questions with end-fall or end-rise intonation to identify which are polite and which are not' ; practising 'minimal pair words … drawn from a recipe or a discussion on cooking from different countries'; listening 'to a simplified weather report in order to identify the number of syllables in familiar words'; and working 'on stressing content words appropriately as part of an activity around giving and responding to instructions'.

Analysis of Reading

The learner read from the introduction to Charles Dickens' 'A Tale of Two Cities'. The book is a Penguin reader containing simplified text at an Upper Intermediate level (level 5). The learner has difficulty in pronouncing the 'th' in '**th**ough', with the pronunciation tending more towards /**t**/. This error is similar to an error he makes in the audio-taped conversation with the 'th' in the word 'thousand'. He also has difficulty in pronouncing the 'th' in 'with', with the pronunciation tending more towards /v/. Both cases are due to the absence of the sound /θ/ in Slavonic languages. The dipthongised /ʊə/ sound in pop**u**lar is pronounced more like the long vowel /uː/. The neutral 'schwa' sound /ə/ in 'Portsm**ou**th' is pronounced more like the diphthong /au/. The long vowel /ɜː/ sound in **ea**rn is pronounced more like the long vowel /i:/. This is due to the fact that the /ɜː/ sound is not found in Slavonic languages. Ironically, the learner mispronounces the 'o' in 'polish', pronouncing it as /əʊ/ rather than /ɒ/. This could be because during parts of the reading, the learner is focussing on one word at a time rather than looking at the context of the sentence.

In general, the learner is correctly able to pronounce words ending in 'ed' e.g. 'helped', 'shaped', 'moved' and 'Determined' i.e. he is able to pronounce the two consonants at the end together. However, with the word 'influenced', the learner pronounces the /e/ sound between the 'c' and the 'd' instead of omitting it and pronouncing the /d/ sound directly after the /s/ sound.

When pronouncing the 'du' in 'education', the learner pronounces /d/ followed by /uː/, but omits the pronunciation of the /j/ sound, which occurs between the two. However, in pronouncing the 'tu' in 'situation', the learner does pronounce the /j/ sound between the two. Monk and Barak (1973) argue that speakers of Slavonic languages have difficulties 'in pronouncing… /d/ … followed by /j/, as in *situation*, *education*… '. However, they also point out that such learners have difficulties with 'the initial clusters /tw/…' and 'pr' although the learner pronounces the words the 'tw' in 'twelve' and the 'pr' in 'prison' correctly.

The learner omits the endings of a couple of words, namely the 'ed' in 'attend**ed**' and the 'ness' in 'hopeless**ness**', and has a lot of difficulty in pronouncing the word 'anxieties'. In each case, the learner could have struggled because of lack of familiarity with the words. The DfES (2001) states that:

> *Adults should learn to*: use a variety of reading strategies to help read and understand an increasing range of unfamiliar words
>
> **DfES (2001: 230)**

The DfES (2001: 231) also suggests some strategies that can be used to achieve this, including; 'visual strategies' where 'words with certain letter patterns' are highlighted; 'structural strategies' where 'words with common suffixes and prefixes in a text' are underlined and their meaning discussed; 'contextual strategies' where 'with guidance, learners use … context to understand' unfamiliar words in a given text and 'the sentence containing the word' and 'phonic strategies' where 'learners identify unfamiliar words, including unfamiliar names, in a narrative'.

It is clear from the way in which the learner reads that he has a good understanding of punctuation. For example he stops at the end of each sentence, and pauses at each comma. This is due to the fact that the learner is literate in his own language, and because, according to Monk and Barak (1987: 121), in Slavonic languages 'punctuation marks and the rules for their use are basically similar to English.'

Writing Sample

The learner was asked to look at the following picture and write a paragraph describing what he could see.

Tower Bridge and HMS Belfast

On the picture we're see Thames River and Tower Bridge.
Tower Bridge was completed in 1894 after 8 years of construction
Tower Bridge is very big strong and beautiful speciall 5o'clock morning when is dark and lights.
On the picture we' ~~are~~ see ships HMS Belfast. I were on the Tower Bridge last week ~~and~~ I crosing to the south side of London in my Lorry

Analysis of Writing Sample

On the first and eighth lines of the written text, the learner writes 'On the picture we've see Thames River/ships HMS Belfast …' instead of '**In** the picture we **can** see the Thames River/the ship HMS Belfast'. It is clear that the learner is not familiar with the use of the modal + infinitive i.e. '*can* + infinitive'. In addition, the learner makes an error relating to subject-verb agreement in writing, 'I were on the …' instead of 'I **was** on the …'. However, the learner uses the past passive tense correctly when he writes 'Tower Bridge was completed in …'. The DfES (2001: 240) states that: '*An adult will be expected to:* use correct basic grammar, e.g. appropriate verb tense, subject-verb agreement' and should 'know that the range/usage of tenses in English does not always correspond directly with the range in learners' other languages, … '. Murphy (1997: 70) offers a range of exercises in order to practice using 'can + infinitive'.

With regard to the use of prepositions, the learner in the above sentences uses 'On' rather than 'In'. In addition the learner writes 'Tower Bridge is … beautiful speciall 5 o'clock morning …' i.e. he omits the preposition 'at' between 'speciall' and '5' and 'in the' between '5 o'clock' and 'morning'. However, he also uses prepositions correctly within the written text e.g. ' … **in** 1894 …', '… crosing **to** the south side **of** London **in** my lorry'. In terms of the use of articles, the learner has, as indicated above, omitted the definite article on two occasions, but has also used it correctly. The reasons for the difficulties that speakers of Slavonic languages have with the use of prepositions and articles, have been outlined above (see analysis of transcribed data – grammar). Murphy (1997) offers a range of exercises in order to practice the use of prepositions and articles.

The learner correctly uses capital letters for proper nouns (e.g. Thames River and HMS Belfast), for the beginning of sentences, and for the pronoun 'I'.

In terms of the learner's spelling, the majority of words in the written text are spelt correctly. However, this could be due to the fact the learner has chosen the words in the written text selectively i.e. has just chosen words that he is familiar with and confident of spelling correctly. The errors that he does make are 'speciall' instead of 'especially' and 'crosing' instead of 'crossing'. The basic and key skill builder communication level 1 workbook 3 for spelling and handwriting (West Nottinghamshire College: 2004) has some clear guidelines (and an exercise) as to how suffixes should be added to verbs, along with a range of other spelling guidelines and accompanying exercises. Workbook 4 contains a range of activities for developing learners' vocabulary. The DfES (2001) suggests a range of strategies for developing learners' spelling and vocabulary, including building up 'word lists of groups of words with common letter patterns and/or sound-symbol associations', 'vocabulary for a particular context', practising 'spelling with gap-fill exercises' and the use of the look – cover – say – write – check method. Where a sound-letter correspondence is being taught, care should be taken to ensure that the learner has an opportunity to hear the sound. Furthermore, when teaching new vocabulary to ESOL learners, the meaning, spoken form of the word and written form of the word should all be emphasised. Writing frames, prepared for a range of levels, can be a useful strategy for developing writing skills in ESOL learners. Examples of writing frames (writing letters, applying for courses etc.) can be found in Spiegel and Sutherland (1999). ESOL learners could also benefit from the support of pictures within the learning materials.). In supporting general English acquisition through the written (and spoken) word, teachers should avoid the danger of overloading the text with unknown words.

On the basis that the learner, as mentioned previously, is generally well educated and literate in his own language, and on the basis that he comes across as a keen and motivated learner, who is currently living and working in the UK and therefore exposed to the English language on a daily basis, the learner is certainly in a position to make improvements in his language and literacy skills (speaking, reading and writing) outlined above.

As mentioned earlier, there are many resources available for developing literacy skills. Likewise, there are many books and resources (some already referred to) available for developing language skills. This book, however, as was also mentioned earlier, is more about providing a framework, and ideas, for developing those skills. Nevertheless, the following resources have been written in order to allow learners the opportunity to practise exercises aimed at developing their speaking, reading and writing skills. The first resource for example focuses on common errors made in everyday spoken English by ESOL learners. Naturally the list can be added to. Although the emphasis of the worksheet is on developing fluency of spoken English, it should be used, through error correction, for developing reading and writing skills also, in the context of the development of one skill reinforcing another. Similarly, the other resources ('Using Prepositions', 'Going to the shops' and 'What do you do in your spare time?') can be used to develop each skill in an integrated context. It should be borne in mind that, as mentioned earlier in the context of developing literacy skills, although the focus of a particular exercise may be on developing an aspect of language, the opportunity can still be taken to address any other issues, whether it be related to pronunciation, grammar or meaning of vocabulary etc. Furthermore, through developing their language skills, ESOL learners should be given the opportunity to develop their literacy skills through, for example, the methods and resources advocated earlier in the book.

ESOL Exercise

Choose and underline the correct form of the verb:

1. Daffodils (grow / are growing) in spring.
2. We (knew / have known) him for 5 years.
3. Jack called while I (worked / was working) on my presentation.
4. Would you like a sandwich? No, thanks, I (have already eaten / ate).
5. Where is Rosie? She (waters / is watering) the plants in the back garden.
6. I cut my finger while I (cooked / was cooking) dinner last night.
7. This is the most beautiful house I (have ever seen / ever saw).
8. Wait for me! I (am coming / come now).
9. I (have not watched / did not watch) 'Gladiator' yet.
10. We (lived / have lived) here since 1998.

Correcting mistakes made in everyday spoken English by ESOL learners

The following sentences contain common errors made in everyday spoken English by ESOL learners. Find the error in each of the following sentences.

1. What does you do for a living? ______
2. I'm teacher in a primary school. ______
3. Do you like you job? ______
4. Does she likes her job? ______
5. She no like him. ______
   Why she no like him? ______
6. He don't go to the maths class very often. ______
7. We went to nice restaurant last night. ______
8. Did you saw that film yesterday? ______
9. Does he has enough money for his train fare? ______
10. I going to London this weekend. ______
11. They don't married yet. ______
12. I did told you about the game didn't I? ______
13. Did you enjoy the film? Yes, I liked. ______

14. What do a mechanic do? A mechanic mends cars.

    ____

15. What do journalists do? A journalists write for newspapers.

    ____

16. What does a nurse do? A nurse look after people in hospital.

    ____

17. Do he go out last night? ______________________________
18. Do you going out later? ______________________________
19. I think he's goes out later on. ______________________________
20. Is he a guy you saw in the pub earlier? ______________________________
21. When you go to the shop, can you get me the pint of milk and a loaf of bread? ______________________________
22. Did you asked him about his new job? ______________________________
23. I've made too much mistakes in this test. ______________________________
24. I have 24 years old. ______________________________
25. The people here is very friendly. ______________________________
26. Everybody know about their problems. ______________________________
27. When you will teach me about English grammar?______________________________
28. Do you know what the solution are?______________________________
29. Those area are quite dangerous.______________________________
30. They haven't announce the train's departure time yet.______________________________

Correcting mistakes made in everyday spoken English by ESOL learners (answers)

1. What **do** you do for a living?
2. I'm **a** teacher in a primary school.
3. Do you like **your** job?
4. Does she **like** her job?
5. She **doesn't** like him. Why **doesn't** she like him?
6. He **doesn't** go to the maths class very often.
7. We went to **a** nice restaurant last night.
8. Did you **see** that film yesterday?
9. Does he **have** enough money for his train fare?
10. **I'm** going to London this weekend.
11. They **aren't** married yet.
12. I did **tell** you about the game didn't I?
13. Did you like the film? Yes, I **did.**
14. What **does** a mechanic do? A mechanic mends cars.
15. What do journalists do? **Journalists** write for newspapers.
16. What does a nurse do? A nurse **looks** after people in hospital.
17. **Did** he go out last night?
18. **Are** you going out later?
19. I think he's **going** out later on.
20. Is he **the** guy you saw in the pub earlier?
21. When you go to the shop, can you get me **a** pint of milk and a loaf of bread.
22. Did you **ask** him about his new job?
23. I've made too **many** mistakes in this test.
24. I **am** 24 years old.
25. The people here **are** very friendly.
26. Everybody **knows** about their problems.
27. When **will you** teach me about English grammar?
28. Do you know what the **solutions** are? *Or* Do you know what the solution **is**?
29. Those **areas** are quite dangerous.
30. They haven't announce**d** the train's departure time yet.

Using Prepositions

Vocabulary (nouns):

ceiling, clock, dustbin, blue cup, blinds, Kevin's wallet, newspaper, TV, register, electric socket, black bag, textbooks, radiator, cupboard, calculator, teacher's desk, posters, CD player, black corduroy jacket

Prepositions:

in front of, behind, opposite, in, on, next to, on top of, under, over, between

Task 1: Working in pairs, and using the vocabulary and prepositions above, take it in turns to ask where objects are in the room.

Example:

Where's the clock?	It's on the wall.
Where are the textbooks?	The textbooks are on the cupboard.

Task 2: Think of three other objects in the room (not written above). Write three questions below, then pass them to a colleague.

Question 1: ....

Answer: ....

Question 2: ....

Answer: ....

Question 3: ....

Answer: ....

Extension activity

Think of another two objects in the room. Write two more questions below, then pass them on to a colleague.

Question 4: ....

Answer: ....

Question 5: ....

Answer: ....

Going to the shops

Vocabulary: Supermarket
some vegetables (carrots and broccoli)
a cabbage and a cauliflower
some bananas
a tin of soup
some washing up liquid
some washing powder
some toilet paper
a bunch of flowers
some coffee
a bag of sugar
a pint of milk
some tomatoes
some potatoes or rice
a loaf of bread

Clothes shop
a shirt
a pair of smart trousers
three T-shirts
a pair of jeans
a pair of shoes
a couple of ties
a black jacket
two pairs of socks
a jumper or a sweater
a dress
a skirt
a raincoat
a warm coat for the winter
an umbrella

The Chemist
a small box of paracetamol
some toothpaste
a bar of soap
some cough mixture
a box of multivitamins
a bottle of shampoo

The Newsagent's
a newspaper (the daily mail or the independent)
a packet of crisps
a can of pepsi or sprite
a bar of chocolate
a box of chocolates
a couple of pens

Speaking exercise

Using the vocabulary above, and working in pairs, take it in turns to be A and B. When you are B, choose at least 3 items (things) from the list.

A. Hi .... , I'm going to **Tesco's/ Sainsbury's/ Matalan/ the supermarket/ the chemists/ the newsagents** to do some shopping**.**
Would you like/ Do you want anything?

B. Yes please, **Can you get me/ I'd like**
.... , ... ,
oh! and ....

Writing exercise

Think of some more items (things) you could buy at the shops above and write them below.

e.g. a large bottle of water, a dictionary, some fruit juice

....

....

....

....

Extension exercise

In pairs, use some of the items you have listed in the speaking exercise above.

What do you do in your spare time?

I play cricket

I tidy the house

What do you **do** in your spare time?

I cook

Speaking Exercise (In Pairs)

A) Hello, I'm .... , what's your name?

B) My name's ....

A) Where are you from?

B) I'm from ....

A) What do you **do** in your spare time?

B) I ....

A) What else do you do in your spare time?

B) I ....

Look at the pictures above.

Picture **1** – What does he do in his spare time? ....

Picture **2** – What does she do in her spare time? ....

What do you like doing in your spare time?

I like playing cricket
I like tidying the house

What do you **like doing** in your spare time?

I like cooking

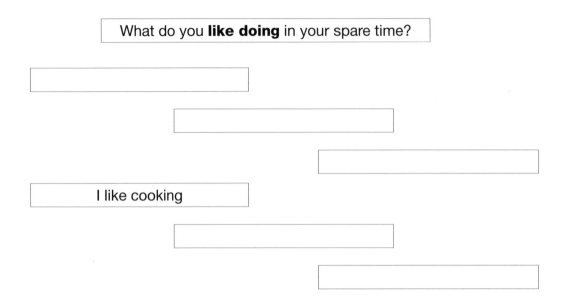

Speaking Exercise (In Pairs)

A) Hello, I'm .... , what's your name?

B) My name's ....

A) Where are you from?

B) I'm from ....

A) What do you like doing in your spare time?

B) I like ....

A) What else do you like doing in your spare time?

B) I like ....

Think again about what you like doing in your spare time. Working in pairs, also talk about things that you **don't** like doing in your spare time.

For example:

A) What do you like doing in your spare time?

B) I like playing football and watching TV, but I don't like jogging or going to the gym.

A) What do you like doing in your spare time?

B) I like .... and .... ,

but I don't like .... or ....

References

Bernstein B (1964) *Elaborated and Restricted codes: Their Origins and Some Consequences,* American Anthropologist Monography issue, Ethnology and Speech.

Brown M (May 14th, 2008) in the Sunday Telegraph

Cameron D (1995) *Verbal Hygiene*, London: Routledge

Carter R, McCarthy M (1997) *Exploring Spoken English*, Cambridge: Cambridge University Press

CBI (2006) *Working on the 3 Rs*, London: DfES

Clark L (Jan 2nd, 2009) in 'The Daily Mail', p1

Department for Education and Skills (2001) *Adult ESOL Core Curriculum*, London: DfES.

Department for Education and Skills (2001) *Adult Literacy Core Curriculum*, London: DfES.

Department for Education and Skills (2003) *Skills for Life, Teacher Reference File,*

Devine J, Carrell PL, Eskey DE (1987) *Research in English as a second language,* Teachers of English to Speakers of Other Languages: Washington DC

Entwhistle H (1978) *Class, Culture and Education,* London: Methuen.

Gagne R (1985) *The Conditions of Learning*, New York: Holt, Rinehart & Winston

Gardiner A (2003) *English Language (A-Level Study Guide)*, Harlow: Pearson Education Limited

Harmer J (1991) *The Practice of English Language Teaching*, Harlow: Longman

Honey J (1997) *Language is Power*, London: Faber and Faber Limited

Hughes A, Trudgill P (1979) *English Accents and Dialects,* London: Edward Arnold Ltd.

Knowles M (1998) *The Adult Learner*, Houston Texas: Gulf Publishing Company

Kramsch C (1998) *Language and Culture*, Oxford: Oxford University Press

Krashen S (1981) *Second Language Acquisition and Second Language Learning*, Oxford: Pergamon Press

Monk B and Burak A (1987) "Russian speakers" in Swan M and Smith B (Eds) *Learner English*, Cambridge: Cambridge University Press

Murphy R (1997) *Essential Grammar in Use*, Cambridge: Cambridge University Press

Richards J and Rodgers T (2001) *Approaches and Methods in Language Teaching*, Cambridge: Cambridge University Press

Smithers R (2006) in *The Guardian*, p1

Spiegel M, Sutherland H (1999) *Writing Works*, London: London South Bank University

Trudgill P (1994) *Dialects*, London: Routledge Limited

Ur P (1984) *Teaching Listening Comprehension*, Cambridge: Cambridge University Press.

Wallace C (1988) *Learning to read in a multicultural society: the social context of second language literacy,* Hemel Hempstead: Prentice Hall

Zera A, Jupp D (2000) 'Widening Participation' in Smithers A, Robinson P (Eds) *Further Education Reformed*, London: Falmer Press pp 129–140